THE DELICATE THREAD

THE DELICATE THREAD

TESHIGAHARA'S LIFE IN ART

Dore Ashton

KODANSHA INTERNATIONAL
Tokyo • New York • London

Published by Kodansha International Ltd., 17-14 Otowa 1-chome, Bunkyo-ku, Tokyo 112, and Kodansha America, Inc.

Distributed in the United States by Kodansha America, Inc., 114 Fifth Avenue, New York, New York 10011, and in the United Kingdom and continental Europe by Kodansha Europe Ltd., 95 Aldwych, London WC2B 4JF.

The publisher would like to thank the Sogetsu-kai Foundation for their assistance.

Library in Congress Cataloguing-in-Publication Data pending.

ISBN 4-7700-1826-6

C O N T E N T S

ACKNOWLEDGMENTS

A great many people were generous with their time and knowledge both in Japan and the United States, and I am grateful to them all. A special thanks to Christopher Blasdel for his sensitive translation and guidance. In Japan, many people received me and I wish to thank them here for their special insights, among them Ichirō Hariu, Shin'ichi Segi, Donald Richie, Kyōko Kishida, Sadamasa Motonaga, Hide Ishiguro, Makoto Oda, Mami Dōmoto, Hisao Dōmoto, Yumi Dōmoto, Arata Isozaki, Noriaki Tsuchimoto, Reiko Kruk, Kuniharu Akiyama, Hideo Kanze, Yoshiaki Inui, Matazō Kayama, Tōru Haga, Kiyoshi Awazu, Issey Miyake, Kyōko Edo, Rentarō Mikuni, Seizō Hayashiya, Yūsuke Nakahara, Shin'ya Izumi and Leslie Pockell. In New York, I thank Paolo Suzuki, Hiroaki Satō, Alexandra Monroe, Linden Chubin, Naoto Nakagawa, Ruri Kawashima, the Japan Society and Barbara Middlebrook.

JAPANESE HISTORICAL PERIODS

PREHISTORIC
Jōmon ca. 10,000 B.C.–ca. B.C. 300
Yayoi ca. 300 B.C.–ca. A.D. 300
Kofun ca. 300–710

ANCIENT
Nara 710–94
Heian 794–1185

MIDDLE AGES (MEDIEVAL)
Kamakura 1185–1333
Northern and Southern Courts 1333–92
Muromachi 1392–1573
Warring States 1482–1573

PREMODERN
Momoyama 1573–1600
Edo 1600–1868

EARLY MODERN / MODERN
Meiji 1868–1912
Taishō 1912–26
Shōwa 1926–1989
Heisei 1989 to present

F O R E W O R D

*T*hroughout his working life Hiroshi Teshigahara has deliberately, perhaps instinctively, chosen paths that lead beyond borders. Boundary markers do not concern him, whether between centuries or geographic regions. For him, they are meant to be crossed. "In art," he maintains, "there must never be any borderlines." He has taken frequent artistic turnings, but always behind them lies a conviction that there is something universal in human experience that he can and must locate and express. "History and cultural problems may change over time but fundamental human problems do not."[1]

Teshigahara is well aware that the world at large will most often examine his works in the light of the oldest conventions governing discussions of Japanese art. Such reflexive conventions assume that there is something Eastern, something fundamentally different about the art of this islandic people, so long confined within borders which they themselves, for centuries, sought to make impenetrable. To some degree, Teshigahara's position is a response to the received ideas of the nature of the arts that happened to have been nurtured in Japan. Some of those ideas have obviously been sponsored by the Japanese themselves, just as some of the more exclusive attitudes in the West have appeared for reasons that often have little to do with artistic experience. I think, for instance, of the artists in my own country who defensively insisted on the American character of their work when threatened by political forces that equated avant-garde with subversive leftism. During the McCarthy era, many artists who basically identified with an international movement known as modernism nonetheless tried to find the hidden elements in their work that could reassure their antagonists that they were true representatives of America. But they knew, as I think all artists know, that the history of art proves that there is no nation that has developed a purely national art.

In the many histories of art from various parts of the world, there are always statements by artists themselves, and by their chroniclers, in which fundamental issues are seen to transcend localities or eras. In 1254 for instance, Tachibana no Narisue wrote a treatise on painting in which he not only proudly declared that "there is nothing that painting cannot render," but added as proof that a painter called Naritsu painted a cock so convincingly that a real cock wanted to fight it.[2] A nearly identical story in the West that every art student encounters holds that an ancient Greek painter could so convincingly render grapes that birds came to peck at them.

Aside from the numerous parallelisms that can be found in discrete histories of the arts, there are also many instances that suggest that no country or region has ever developed its artistic tradition from a single point of view. In Tachibana's thirteenth-century Japan, for example, there were different viewpoints. His vaunted realism was countered by the speculations of the great Zen authority Musō Soseki (Musō Kokushi 1275–1351)—monk, artist, scholar, and politician. Musō wrote a treatise reviewing temporal art and culture, and concluded: "All this is but a dream within a dream."[3] A few centuries later, the Confucian scholar Arai Hakuseki (1675–1725) complained about the profusion of non-rational historians saying that "the history of our country is turning into an account of dreams told in a dream."[4] The idea of the dream within a dream has a venerable history in the West, also, and during Hakuseki's era, occurs frequently in Europe, and most particularly in Spain, in poetry and plays. It is vividly evoked in Calderon's great line: "La vida es sueño y sueños sueños son."

In our own century there are innumerable examples of shared human preoccupations occurring spontaneously in different cultures. There is a stunning illustration in a paragraph from the twentieth-century Japanese author Natsume Sōseki (1867–1916) in his novel, *The Gate*. Soseki's protagonist comes to a Zen temple:

> He had come to the gate and asked to have it opened. The bar was on the other side and when he knocked, no one came.

He heard a voice saying, "Knocking will do no good. Open it yourself." He stood there and wondered how he could open it. He thought clearly of a plan, but he could not find the strength to put it into effect. . . . He was never meant to pass through it, nor was he meant to be content until he was allowed to do so. He was, then, one of the most unfortunate beings who must stand by the gate, unable to move, and patiently waiting for the day to end.[5]

Soseki might have been inspired by the thirteenth-century Chinese classic, *Wu-men Kuan (The Gateless Gate)*, or he might have invented his allegory drawing on his own experiences or those of other dispirited twentieth-century thinkers, or from his own idiosyncratic, melancholy cast of mind that always brought him to a threshold but never beyond. Surely Franz Kafka in the twentieth century knew nothing of Soseki when he wrote of K. whose gatekeeper in effect said that knocking would do him no good. There is nothing in Kafka's history to suggest that he had ever delved seriously into Chinese literature or Japanese Zen, nor even Jewish Kabala, in which there are certain common features with Zen Buddhism.

In the astonishing Japanese classic, often called the first psychological novel in the world, *The Tale of Genji*, Murasaki Shikibu discusses the source of the novelist's impetus. She has Genji say:

It happens because the storyteller's own experience of men and things, whether for good or ill—not only what he has passed through himself but even events which he has only witnessed or been told of—has moved him to an emotion so passionate that he can no longer keep it shut up in his heart. Again and again something in his own life or in that around him will seem to the writer so important that he cannot bear to let it pass into oblivion. There must never come a time, he feels, when men do not know about it.[6]

The passion Lady Murasaki describes is what drives artists in any part of the world, in any country or continent. In the work of such artists we can recognize ourselves. When Teshigahara insists that he is seeking the artistic language that knows no boundaries, he is admitting into his universe of visual art the *gaijin*, the "outside person," who most often is unaware of his particular background, and of the many specialized terminologies that distinguish the history of Japanese art.

Perhaps Teshigahara's distinct personal history will help to illuminate his choices along the way, but it does not explain his persistent pursuit of forms in which all the arts participate—a genre favored in the twentieth century with a history going back to Wagner's *Gesamtkunstwerk*, or total work of art. Even this nineteenth-century tradition has precedents, but in its twentieth-century advent, it assumed new forms. Historically speaking, however, the total work of art in the West was not inherently different from its counterparts in the East. In fact, it often drew upon precepts encountered in Eastern experiments. The Russian avant-garde theater just before and just after the Revolution was often inspired by studies of theater in China, India, and Japan. Avant-garde Russian film was enriched when Sergei Eisenstein discovered Kabuki theater and recognized it as the perfect prototype of the total work of art. "The sharpest distinction between Kabuki and our theater," he wrote, "is—if such an expression may be permitted—in a monism of ensemble."[7] The profound impression made on Eisenstein by a visiting Kabuki troupe was translated into new theater and film techniques that would in turn influence Japanese artists, most of whom were aware of Eisenstein's important essay on Kabuki.

In Teshigahara's own background there is a tradition of total art going back to the medieval period and the teachings of Musō Soseki. In Musō's recorded thoughts there is always a stress on the role of intuition. He urged his followers to explore the concept of the garden as a perfect compendium of sensations, materials, sounds, colors, movements, and elemental forces that were to be drawn into a single work of art. Musō's teachings remained vital and were extensively used by twentieth-century artists such as Isamu Noguchi, and by Teshigahara himself. But not exclusively: there were countless other initiatives by artists both in Japan, Europe, and the United States encountered by Teshigahara that helped to form his personal culture. In whatever he has undertaken there is a clear temperamental preference for what Eisenstein called the "monistic ensemble." Teshigahara is by nature gregarious and likes to perform in ensembles or direct them. He likes collaborations, and he has a natural gift for organizing multifarious activities. Almost everything he has done attests to his unconcern with conventional limitations of genre or medium. The complex issues that have often tormented twentieth-century Japanese artists have not left Teshigahara untouched, but they are addressed by him with a certain jauntiness— a kind of devil-may-care attitude that spares him the paralysis of Soseki's anti-hero caught in his Hamletic soul at the threshold of the gate.

Nearly always the most vexing question posed by modern Japanese artists to themselves is the question of what is uniquely Japanese in Japanese art. The labyrinthine arguments constituting a genre of Japanese criticism have certainly occurred to Teshigahara, but they have never inhibited him. He is careful to avoid the snares of rhetoric and to preserve his status as a working artist, not a theoretician. He has shown that he is ready at most moments in his life to change course. Practicing several arts in the various cycles of his life, Teshigahara might in Western terminology be called "a Renaissance man."

Throughout his artistic career, Teshigahara has consistently held on to certain principles and convictions, one of the most important being his belief that everyone is endowed with a creative instinct. A child brought to the beach, he points out, commences to build sand castles. In the opening scene in Teshigahara's first full length film, *Pitfall*, his camera focuses on a thin, grubby child, the son of an impoverished

A Scene from Pitfall *emphasizing the "feeling of clay."*

Scene from Rikyū; *Rikyū examining a teabowl.*

miner, who plays concentratedly with mud, fashioning small, sculptural shapes—one of many scenes in Teshigahara's films showing human hands at work, inventing. Years later Teshigahara himself became enchanted with clay and would describe his embarkation as a potter in such a way as to emphasize his point concerning the most basic creative instinct at work in everyone: "I was attracted by *earth*, not the art of pottery. I wanted the *feeling* of clay." The solemn boy in *Pitfall*, deprived of all enriching privileges, nonetheless instinctively fashions the mud surrounding his hut into objects. Subsequently, in almost all of Teshigahara's films, there were incidental scenes of people making things, either artistic things such as ceramic bowls, as in *Rikyū*, or ordinary things, such as humble but carefully prepared meals.

An innate respect for natural creativity has threaded through Teshigahara's life and is the most consistent element in his many activities as filmmaker, ceramist, calligrapher, designer, opera director, or impresario of avant-garde activities. From the elemental desire to shape mud to the sophisticated wish to orchestrate a tea ceremony, Teshigahara quite consciously strives to preserve intact the purity of his first impulse, which he regards as the origin of all creativity and the source of the possibility that there is a universal human experience.

Note: All quotations not mentioning sources are from conversations or interviews with the author.

NOTES

1   Peter Grilli, "After 17 Years, a Director Reappears," *The New York Times*, Sept. 24, 1989, p. H15.

2   Vera Linhartova, *Sur un Fond Blanc*, Paris, INALCO, 1993, p. 127.

3   Musō Soseki (Musō Kokushi), quoted in *Irmtrand Schaarschmidt Richter* and Osamu Mori, *Japanese Gardens*, New York, 1979, p. 59.

4   Arai Hakuseki, *Sources of Japanese Tradition*, Vol. I, compiled by Ryūsaku Tsunoda, W. Theodore de Bary, and Donald Keene, New York, 1964, p. 465.

5   Natsume Sōseki, from *The Gate*, cited by Edwin McClellan in the introduction to *Grass by the Wayside*, Tokyo, 1989, p. viii.

6   Murasaki Shikibu (Lady Murasaki), *The Tale of Genji*, trans. Arthur Waley, in *Sources of Japanese Tradition*, Vol. I, compiled by Ryusaku Tsunoda, W. Theodore de Bary, and Donald Keene, New York, 1964, p. 178.

7   Sergei Eisenstein, *Film Form, Essays in Film Theory*, New York, 1949, p. 20.

Bamboo installation by Teshigahara. March 1996. Kennedy Center, Washington, D.C.

Ballet Girl *by Teshigahara. 1950. Oil on canvas, 145 x 112 cm. Artist's collection.*

Lunch by *Teshigahara. 1950. Oil on canvas, 112 x 145 cm. Artist's collection.*

Garden designed by Teshigahara. 1985. Ken Domon Museum of Photography, Yamagata Prefecture. ▶

Teshigahara working with clay. 1980. Echizen, Fukui Prefecture.

Fired Echizen ceramics.

Teshigahara arranging flowers in a ceramic vessel of his own design.

A finished arrangement.

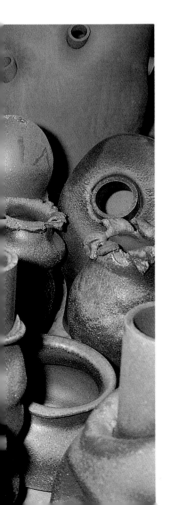

◄ Bamboo installation by Teshigahara. 1982. Shiseido Art House, Kakegawa-shi, Shizuoka Prefecture.

◄ Bamboo installation by Teshigahara. 1993. Naoshima Contemporary Art Museum, Naoshima, Kagawa Prefecture.

Bamboo stage set by Teshigahara for the 1923 Noh-style play
The Woman and Her Shadow *by Paul Claudel. 1993. Paris.*

Two scenes from the opera Turandot *with bamboo stage sets by Teshigahara. 1996. Geneva.* ▶

◄ *Bamboo installation by Teshigahara. December 1989 to January 1990. One-man show at the National Museum of Contemporary Art, Seoul.*

◄ *Bamboo installation by Teshigahara. 1987. Sogetsu Plaza, Tokyo.*

Visitors passing through bamboo installation by Teshigahara. March 1996. Kennedy Center, Washington, D.C.

Teshigahara at Kennedy Center.

1

The first postwar generation to which Teshigahara belongs felt an urgent need to assert itself, to start from degree zero to build a radically different view of the world. Most of Teshigahara's artistic colleagues, and he himself, had been educated almost entirely during the most repressive years of the Japanese military regime. With one or two exceptions, Teshigahara's comrades in art school and in the important years of their first essays into the arts, were too young to have been drafted when the Second World War erupted but not too young to have been rounded up for war service during the last desperate year. When they resumed their education they were faced at every turn with moral and physical ruin. Tokyo itself was glutted with rubble. The reorganization of the most basic services required in urban life was chaotic. The artistic milieu festered with bitter conflicts. Slightly older artists accused each other of collaboration, while younger artists denounced them and everything that had existed in prewar Japan. Even the survivors of a far earlier period, when the arts of the avant-garde had had a brief florescence just after the First World War, were looked upon with suspicion. Their nostalgic reminiscences often fell upon deaf ears among the young.

The poets, musicians, filmmakers, and painters in the group to which Teshigahara gravitated—many of whom are friends and collaborators to this day—had diverse experiences of the war and differing family backgrounds, but almost without exception, they were determined to renounce not only their brief personal pasts but also the entire Japanese ethos as they had learned to perceive it as "military boys" in their teens. As artists in their early twenties, they were determined to invent a new Japan. For Teshigahara this was not an easy task. He had had a significantly privileged childhood. Unlike his friends, he had been exposed to a powerful artistic figure—his father, Sōfū—whose reputation as an unorthodox artist was as well established as his social position as *iemoto*, or head, of a flourishing school of flower arranging. This towering figure cast a very large shadow within which his artistically-inclined son sheltered. Sōfū himself had been the son of a rather rebellious figure. His father Hisatsugu, known as Wafū, had come to Tokyo soon after Sōfū was born, around 1902 or 1903, where he installed himself in a European-style house—a gesture that declared his defiance of the standard life-style of an ikebana master—and established his institute for flower arranging. Based on Sōfū's recollections, historians have described Wafū as a "rationalist" who, in teaching ikebana, developed a system offering geometric indications of where and how sprigs and flowers should be placed—something unheard of in those days and harshly criticized within the hierarchical ikebana establishment.

Wafū emerges as a quirky eccentric in Sōfū's account of his youth. Not only did he object to Sōfū's wanting to go to high school but also declared that he could understand permitting children with poor minds to enter a school in order to study, but failed to understand why children with good minds should. Accordingly, Sōfū was given a classic literati education and lessons in ikebana by his strong-willed father. Sōfū later vouchsafed a telling detail to an interviewer from *Time* magazine. He related that when he turned eighteen, he rebelled, inventing an ikebana of his own and declaring to his father that it represented "an extension of his individualism." Wafū slapped his face. Individualism could go only so far in Wafū's world, and certainly, like most Japanese during the late Taishō and early Shōwa periods, Wafū felt uneasy with assertive individualists. Seven years later the friction between father and son became intolerable, and the father expelled Sōfū from the family enterprise.

By the time Hiroshi was born six months later, Sōfū had already established his own school, Sōgetsu—meaning grass and moon—in which he assumed the traditional role of *iemoto*. For an outspoken "individualist," this was something of a paradox and may have been born of economic necessity. But I suspect that for a man with a driving ambition to dominate, as Sōfū certainly wished to do, the role of *iemoto* was not only convenient, it was essential to success. Traditionally the *iemoto*—which literally means "head of household"—controlled many practitioners who emerged from his studio. Not only was an *iemoto* granted enormous prestige, but he garnered inordinate economic advantages. His organization was hierarchical: he collected fees from granting diplomas, for instruction, and for membership in the specific school. Using these advantageous resources, Sōfū, who seemed intent on using the system to subvert the system, lived a double life: on the one hand, he was chief executive of an enterprise that provided a generous income, and on the other he was an extravagantly experimental vanguard artist.

This situation brought considerable criticism but also considerable attention. *Time* magazine, for instance, did not fail to report in 1978 that the aging master travelled in a chauffeured white Cadillac and owned a Western-style house in Tokyo "that reportedly cost $830,000." By this time, Sōfū had become chief of what his detractors always called an empire, with more than a million dues-paying members all over the world. Even during Hiroshi's childhood, Sōfū had provided his family with a comfortable life in what Hiroshi fondly recalls as a "three-storied house my father built in Kojimachi-Sanbancho, that even as a child I could tell was very refined and modern, and quite conspicuous by its style in Tokyo at that time." Sōfū's other life transpired in the works which won him standing outside of the traditional Japanese school mode, and recognition by other visual artists as an experimental anomaly in the world of formal ikebana.

The circumstances in which Sōfū's generation matured were hardly propitious. Nearly every artist coming of age in the 1920s was met with pressing problems that had their sources largely outside of the artists' personal lives. These historical circumstances figure strongly in any approach to the generation to which Hiroshi belongs. Much of this generation's youthful energy was expended in the difficult assessment of the situation of its childhood. It was crucial to look back in order to understand what had brought the Japanese to the catastrophe these young artists had witnessed. The countless youth groups that rose from the ashes of the war considered knowing prewar history essential to the understanding of their own lives.

Hiroshi was no exception. His thoughts about prewar Japan begin

Hiroshi Teshigahara, at 13, with his family in Tokyo, 1940. From left to right: Kasumi (younger sister), grandmother, younger cousin, Hiroshi, mother, and aunt.

Sōgetsu Kōdō (Hall) in Kōji-machi, Tokyo, near Teshigahara's childhood home.

with the unacceptable fact that during his childhood "everything was in a vertical order." The task for his generation, as he and his friends saw it, was to overthrow the "traditional" hierarchies that persisted on so many levels in Japanese life. In animated discussions these young artists searched in political history for answers to questions not only present in their personal artistic lives but also in their civic lives. Above all, they concerned themselves with the zigzagging history of Japanese cultural nationalism.

To the young, cultural nationalism seemed to have been born with the Meiji Restoration (1868) and reborn with each subsequent generation. There was always an upsurge of patriotic conservatism each time Japan had embarked on military adventures, as when they won the war against China in 1895 and the war with Russia in 1905. Between 1906 and 1912, there was acute political unrest that in many ways set the tone for the entire period preceding the Second World War. The defeat of Russia was decisive in late Meiji history. The government, armed with a flexible and less than democratic constitution, felt confident enough to undertake a campaign against what the law called "dangerous thoughts"—a sinister phantom law that brought many tragic deaths—rooting out dissident elements, imprisoning extremely young radicals who had modeled their groups on Russian precedents, and in notorious cases, executing them. In the aftermath of the Russo-Japanese War, state textbooks on ethics were redrafted, Shintō and the emperor cult entered into the curricula, and rural youth groups were subject to mass ideological mobilization. Press laws were passed, censorship controls radically tightened, novelists brought to trial for obscenity (while popular traditional "erotic books," as a fantasy outlet, were left untouched), revolutionaries imprisoned, and in the case of the Kōtoku Shūsui "plot" against the Emperor, executed en masse.[1]

Those first purges of the century were followed by another after the 1923 earthquake that was quite successful in intimidating dissenters. The most vital art community lived in Tokyo, which was physically devastated in the quake. Taking advantage of the chaos that prevailed, the government allegedly authorized murderous sorties against radical groups, and there were deaths and internments. Sōfū's school got underway shortly after the notorious 1925 Peace Preservation Act that ushered in the Shōwa period. Although the new law guaranteed male suffrage, it granted little else. It enhanced the power of the Higher

Special Police and made it a crime to advocate any changes in the government system, in capitalism, or in the constitution. A contemporary writer, Seikichi Fujimori mocked the Act's treatment of civil liberties, which, he said, meant in effect, "We grant you freedom of expression. However, you have no right to express what has been prohibited."[2] Progressive writers and activists nonetheless expressed their dissatisfaction with the new laws for a time, but as the worldwide depression deepened from 1929 onward, Japan's government became increasingly authoritarian and aggressive, making its first move toward Asian conquest in 1931 in Manchuria.

Despite the repressive implications of the Peace Preservation Act, Japan continued to offer the world a benign image. In the year that Sōfū opened his school, a lecturer was dispatched to Columbia University to proffer the standard Japanese self-image of *Present Day Japan*, as the published lectures were called. The professor, Yūsuke Tsurumi, tendered the received idea of the Japanese national character: "The Japanese have a curious aversion to extremity. Moderation is the virtue we cherish, sometimes to an immoderate degree." Tsurumi described the outstanding Japanese trait as the "love of harmony" and offered the government's authorized views on the main differences between East and West as deriving from their different attitudes toward harmony. "Individual liberty has been accentuated in the West and it is undoubtedly the foundation of Western progress, while in the East, at least in Japan, the foundation of moral ideas has been harmony." These unchallenged views sanctioned by an increasingly military government were impressed on the public and effectively stifled a burgeoning avant-garde as Japan edged toward total conflagration.

Sōfū's youthful declaration of "individualization" flew in the face of the prevailing official sentiment. It was a pugnacious stance that he carried out in his work and in the principles he laid down for his school. Traditional values were bluntly refused in his pedagogy, which, considering that he functioned in a society that largely submitted to rules and restrictions, testified to his strength of purpose.

At the same time, as the military began to make life more and more uncomfortable for members of progressive views in the cultural sphere, there was a noticeable rise in nostalgia for ancient ways. Even artists who had begun with the firm resolve to absorb Western ideas, at least those distinguishing the modern movements in literature and art, began

THE
DELICATE
THREAD
•
38

to cast their eyes back to other Japanese eras which represented more satisfying aesthetic conditions—or at least they liked to think so. Their reconsideration of haiku, calligraphy, and classic Japanese novels was perhaps encouraged by a wave of Westerners who, reacting to the postwar chaos in Europe, came to Japan seeking traditions that had remained intact. In ikebana they found the traditional approach well preserved. The wife of the German author Eugen Herrigel, whose book *Zen in the Art of Archery* became an important Western source on Zen Buddhism during the 1930s and immediately after the war, published her own book based on her experience studying with an ikebana master. It appeared with a fulsome preface by Daisetz Suzuki—the author who most influenced Western perceptions of Zen—in which he wrote:

> The Western mind has been coarsened by the technique of exact analysis, whereas the Eastern mind is pre-eminently mystical and concerns itself with the so-called mystery of existence.[3]

Mrs. Herrigel fervently believed this view of the so-called Eastern mind (as did far too many others, ignorant of the opposing views present throughout Japanese history and also of the shifting positions of officials throughout its history). She wrote reverently of her experience with the Zen ikebana master, Bokyo Takeda, during the late 1920s, describing what she called "the summons to mindfulness" the master demanded:

> One can well say that the "inner work" of flower arrangement must keep pace with the outer. Only so can it be a wholeness of heaven, man and earth. The hour for arranging the flowers pervades the entire day; it does not stand outside.[4]

She concludes her book:

> That which underlies the art and needs to be experienced is itself formless, but it takes on form as soon as you try to represent it symbolically. . . . The flowers are not brought into harmony by looking at them first from one side and then the other, by experimenting and comparing—only the beginner does that—rather the eye is directed inwards. Not the slightest

intention of arranging them "beautifully" must disturb this self-immersion, not even the desire to become "purposeless on purpose."[5]

This mystical approach was far from Sōfū's mind when he formulated his own principles. Hiroshi's view of his father's originality stresses Sōfū's strong interest in modernity. He points out that ikebana's 500-year history originating from samurai practices evolved in relation to the architecture of each era. His father took the radical step of removing flower arrangements from the traditional *tokonoma*—the niche designed in traditional houses to hold flower arrangements and painting—in order to keep up with Western architecture. "The motto of Sōgetsu to this day is based on Sōfū's vision: Ikebana has to evolve corresponding to the times, in any space, with any material." Since Sōfū was a sculptor, calligrapher, and painter, as well as an ikebana adept, the famous three-story house was more than a school. Hiroshi's earliest impressions were gleaned from his father's large collection of art books and catalogues. Before he ever got to art school he had, in his mind's eye, a cache of images drawn from books on Impressionism, Post-Impressionism, Dadaism, deStijl, and Cubism, as well as from books on the traditional arts of Japan. Sōfū's undertaking—to transform an ancient artistic practice into a modern one—required that he look beyond the unvarying routines of traditional art. Like other progressive artists in the 1920s and 1930s, he felt, as he said, shackled by the constant recourse to ancient models. Many artists of his generation threw off the weight of tradition by fleeing to Paris or sometimes to the United States. Sōfū remained in Japan but carefully followed the accounts, both written and verbal, of his travelling artistic colleagues.

A few of these colleagues, so adamant in their belief in modernism, would later figure importantly in postwar activities. During their wander years, they had broadcast their discoveries regularly in the magazines between the wars, and in a few instances, had written celebrated books. Shūzō Takiguchi (1903–1979), who was important in initiating Teshigahara's generation to modernist ideas, had thoroughly explored Paris. As an active participant in André Breton's Surrealist movement he gained an intimate knowledge of Parisian vanguard ideas which he enthusiastically transmitted to Japan. Within months of its publication in Paris, he translated Breton's *Surrealism and Painting* in 1930. Saburō

Hasegawa (1906–1957) was also a prolific commentator as well as a painter. He had visited the United States in 1929, and in 1930 ensconced himself in Paris where he vigorously participated in the organization Abstraction-Création, founded in 1931. In 1937, the year the second Sino-Japanese war commenced, Hasegawa published an influential book, *Abstract Art*, in which he considered the works of artists he had known in Paris, including Piet Mondrian, Wassily Kandinsky, and Hans Arp, and sought to make certain parallels with the work of early Japanese painters such as Sesshū (1420–1506). Both Takiguchi and Hasegawa, during the perilous years of the military ascent when every aspect of Japanese life was under brutal surveillance, were increasingly preoccupied with questions of identity. They were among the first artists to reject cultural nationalism, but they were also among the first to look back, seeking in older Japanese traditions, and especially in artistic practices influenced by Zen Buddhism, tendencies toward individual freedom that they could equate with their own. These thoughtful artists would become the mentors of Teshigahara's generation.

By natural inclination Teshigahara was open to all forms of art. In his early high school years he had frequented Noh and Kabuki theaters and had taken up Taiko drumming. By the time he entered art school, he had had considerable exposure to both classical and modern art, but he enrolled at first in the section of traditional painting, which he soon found unsatisfying. He was spared further traditional studies by the war. Unlike many extremely young Japanese during the last phases of the war, Teshigahara was not drafted for active service, largely, he says, because his records had been bombed out of existence. But along with other friends in art school, he was enlisted to support the war effort. They were sent to Ōshima in Yamaguchi Prefecture where they worked as illustrators for textbooks for students in the army and navy. It was there, not very far from Hiroshima, that they experienced the reverberations of the first atomic bomb.

Although Teshigahara is reluctant to talk about that crucial experience, and when he does, he speaks briefly, the appearance of the mushroom cloud was to remain with him and was far more important than the physical shock of the explosion. One of his recent collaborators, now a faithful friend, Reiko Kruk, a makeup specialist, recalls talking with Teshigahara about those dreadful moments. She describes how Teshigahara, a few years later, visited a hospital in Nagasaki, and viewing a victim, fainted.

"He is a man who understands the pain of others." In his own terse account of the 1945 catastrophe, Teshigahara relates that he returned to Tokyo four or five days after the surrender with thoughts only of death.

Whole quarters had disappeared in the Tokyo to which Teshigahara returned, including his childhood neighborhood near the Imperial Palace. The nearly total devastation of everything familiar cast a pall on the spirits of the young artists who understood all too well that no one in the immediate postwar era could be exempt from the hideous legacy of the war. The society to which Teshigahara returned was not only prostrate, it was inchoate and excessively vulnerable. The writer Yoshie Hotta (1918–) soon attempted to characterize the period in *Hōjōki Shiki*, (Notes on *Hōjōki*). The title refers to the celebrated work of the Kamakura period by Kamo no Chōmei (1153–1216), the *Hōjōki*, or *An Account of a Ten-Foot Square Hut*, written in the same period as the *Tale of the Heike*. Chōmei reflected the turbulence and disorder of his lifetime by describing endless disasters both natural and devised by man, in a deeply pessimistic tone. Hotta attempts to describe the profound effects of the atomic disaster. In one scene he characterizes dispirited people sifting through the ruins. On the day the Emperor appears, they grovel ignominiously and beg forgiveness for the disaster. To enforce his narrative, Hotta mixes in phrases from the *Hōjōki*, such as, "The old capital was already deserted, the new yet to be completed. People all felt like drifting clouds." Hotta's contemporaries, when the Emperor appears, "prostrated themselves in damp ashes . . . Dazzled by the shining car and shining boots, they were taking the blame for what happened." His indignation before this humiliating spectacle knows no bounds:

> More than a hundred thousand people killed or injured in air raids of just one night and they thought not of the survivors, but of death, oriented everything toward death—what is this? . . . There must have been something in Japanese thought down through the ages that had kept death and not life at the center of human existence . . . [6]

Hotta bitterly denounces this old Japanese habit of mind which he lays at the door of Buddhism. He speaks of the "politicization" of the Buddhist idea of the impermanent, transient nature of all things, writing that, "The ruling class as well as the victims of the disaster lay the blame on 'impermanence' when there is no place else to lay it." For example, in time of disaster, Kamo no Chōmei described people saying:

Having no wings we cannot fly up to the sky.
One who follows the ways of the world may suffer.
One who does not seems mad.

Hotta concludes that there is a need to try "to excavate what lives and lies heavy across the roots of our spiritual and intellectual life."[7] While few in Teshigahara's circle were prepared to excavate to the depths that Hotta describes, many were uneasily aware of Japanese cultural patterns that might obstruct their own will to build anew.

When Teshigahara and his friends returned to Tokyo to scenes of unimaginable suffering and confusion, they were obviously in no mood to accept the passive wisdom of which Hotta so passionately complained. The years of deprivation of contact with other peoples weighed heavily on them. They were filled with consternation, and in some cases, loathing for their own past, and they strove to fill in the gaping lacunae in their own educations as swiftly as possible. The postwar intellectual climate vibrated with questions, above all questions about the Japanese self-image as "harmonious." The reappearance of long-censored commentaries reminded them that it was not "harmony" that had incited the rice riots early in the century, or the formation of leftist groups, so quickly cut down, all through the first half of the century. They were keenly aware that as artists and writers not aligned with government bureaucracy, they bore the burden of dissent and independent thought.

NOTES

1   Peter N. Dale, *The Myth of Japanese Uniqueness*, New York, 1986, p. 206.

2   Gregory J. Kasza, *The State and the Mass Media in Japan*, Berkeley, 1993, p. 47

3   Gustie Herrigel, *Zen in the Art of Flower Arranging*, London, 1958, pp. xi–xii.

4   Ibid., p. 18.

5   Ibid., p. 120.

6   Yoshie Hotta, *Hōjōki Shiki*, trans. Jane Corddry, *LOTUS*, Vol. 55, 1984 (Afro-Asian Conference).

7   Ibid.

2

*D*uring the immediate postwar years, the intellectuals, as Masao Maruyama remarked, formed a "community of contrition."[1] Everybody in the arts belonged to that community, and according to critic Shin'ichi Segi, became extreme in one way or another. Those who, like the composer Tōru Takemitsu (1930–96), a friend of Teshigahara's, had been deprived of the arts of the enemy as officially decreed, became enthusiastic explorers in the culture of the enemy. Takemitsu had been only fourteen when he was drafted into the student labor forces. His early memories of the war included an inundation with classical Japanese music which later "always recalled the bitter memories of the war."[2] Later he would recount his important first encounter with Western music. One day an officer in the remote barracks where the young recruits were working took them to his headquarters and, using a carefully sharpened piece of bamboo for a needle, played Josephine Baker singing "Parlez-Moi d'Amour." It was then, Takemitsu wrote, that he first responded to the "splendid quality of Western music."[3] When he was demobilized, he turned his back on classical Japanese musical traditions and for more than fifteen years assiduously steeped himself in Western modernism.

His deep sense of disgrace as a Japanese was characteristic of his whole group of artistic acquaintances, including Teshigahara. When Teshigahara returned to the Tokyo School of Fine Arts (Tokyo Bijutsu Gakkō, now Tokyo Geijutsu Daigaku), he shunned the traditional section and enrolled in the Western department that had been entirely overhauled. Most of the new professors had been abroad in the inter-war years and regarded themselves as part of the international modern art movement. Among them were Ryūzaburō Umehara (1888–1986) and Kokei Kobayashi (1883–1957), both of whom were budding artists in the prewar period. All the same, Teshigahara recalls that period in his education somewhat ruefully. "Certainly they were wonderful compared to the previous teachers who were extremely academic, but I still felt strongly that something was lacking."

What was lacking, as it turned out, was the voice of a scourge. The students craved a drastic denunciation of the past, and they would find it in the voice of Tarō Okamoto (1911–96), whom Teshigahara always credits as his primary influence during the first decade after the war. Okamoto's style was passionate, provocative, even hectoring. He addressed the young art students in a spirited and uncompromising tone that often shocked them. Yoshikuni Iida, who was then a student, recalled a lecture that Okamoto delivered in 1948 in which he exhorted them "to destroy everything with monstrous energy like Picasso's in order to reconstruct the Japanese art world."[4] Most shocking to Iida was Okamoto's attack on one of his favorite teachers, Umehara, who like Oka-moto, had been in Paris before the war. Okamoto, much like Jarry's Ubu, who declared "we must destroy everything, even the ruins," was

Tarō Okamoto, 1950s.

more than willing to put even his own past into question. He strode into the postwar mess bearing the banner of nonconformity, even to the principles that had fueled previous vanguard traditions which he knew very well, having gone to Paris while still in his teens. He had remained in Paris from 1929 to 1940, and alongside his artistic activities, studied ethnology at the Sorbonne. Like Hasegawa, he gravitated toward the two most vigorous groupings of artists in the 1930s: the Surrealists, and the artists who formed the association that favored abstract artists, Abstraction-Création.

While Abstraction-Création was formally dedicated to the promotion of "non-figurative" art, it was broadly enough construed so that artists with Surrealist proclivities such as Okamoto's friend and mentor, Kurt Seligmann, found a pre-eminent place in its roster. When Okamoto joined the group in 1933, he was the only Japanese and the youngest member. Evidence of his status as an active member are found in the group's publications from 1934 through 1936, in which there were always one or two reproductions of his work and written statements such as, "precisely, one must realize forms that are not forms and colors that are not colors."[5] His Surrealist approach to aesthetics is still more pronounced in 1936:

> Abstract art was for contemporary youth the means of escaping from surrounding reality, the means of replacing it with pure forms and colors and lyrical visions.
> And if the eyes saw only the color or joy, they were no longer eyes. They were beacons.
> Reality is the perpetual expression of vital movement; pictorial reality is the permanent revolution of the human vision.[6]

This statement, redolent of the diction of André Breton, appeared during the same year Okamoto exhibited, thanks to Breton, in the International Surrealist Exhibition. There were differences between the two groups. Abstraction-Création was committed to an artistic revolution. Breton and his friends repeatedly stressed the necessity for the individual artist to adopt a firm political stance. In Breton's view, an artist could not be fully creative without an ethical commitment to social justice. Okamoto was apparently deeply impressed when, with the outbreak of the Spanish Civil War, the Surrealist artists immediately rallied to the Republican cause. His well-known painting of 1936, *Wounded Arm*, is often interpreted in the light of political issues. He wrote later that this painting was his major departure from pure abstraction: "I imagined that a floating ribbon was suddenly made into a bow. Wounded time, tolerating reality, clenched its fist." The clenched fist, symbol of radical political movements, became an inner symbol for Okamoto, who carried it into his vigorous organizing activities after the war. It was he who brought into his postwar discussion groups the idea, broached originally in the brief and disrupted history of the early twentieth-century Japanese vanguard, of "total art."

Okamoto had no doubt encountered artists who had participated in the hectic activities of the *Mavo* and *Sanka* groups between 1923 and 1925, before he left for Paris. These artists had been invigorated by news from Germany, France, and the Soviet Union—news of heteroclitic activities by artists variously associated with Dada, Constructivism, and Futurism. In the mid-1920s, the umbrella group, Sanka, staged the works of the most extravagant iconoclasts and stressed the importance of collaborations. The activities of Sanka extended to the domains of theater and cinema, publicity posters and architectural projects. Its animators organized manifestations which tended toward the union of all genres in a sort of *Gesamtkunstwerk*.

When Okamoto addressed himself to the new generation after the war, he carried with him the experiences of his own youth, but added bitter anecdotes to useless nostalgia. His restless young listeners received him with respect, not only because of his avant-garde credentials, but because he was thought to have been a victim of the secret police, who considered that he harbored "dangerous thoughts," and arranged to have him sent into the war as a common soldier. By 1948, Okamoto was active with people who were later called *Sengoha*, the "après guerre" generation. He formed *Yoru no Kai* (Night Group), which was specifically devoted to the creation of what he called "total art." This group quickly bifurcated, and its youngest members, among them Kōbō Abe and the poet Hiroshi Sekine, founded *Seiki no Kai* (Group of the Century). It was in this group that Okamoto's theories were most avidly discussed and found expression in works of art. Okamoto had stated his basic view in embryo in 1948, when he noted that the two dominant modern movements, both of which he had participated in, were diametrically opposed. Abstract painting, he said, was inorganic and rational, while

TESHIGAHARA'S
LIFE
IN ART
•
47

Members of Seiki no Kai *(Group of the Century), including Kōbō Abe (front row, left), Teshigahara (front row, center), and Shin'ichi Segi (back row, right). December 1950.*

Surrealist painting was irrational. He proposed that both tendencies be accepted in their tension as opposites, in their "violently dissonant relations." How deeply Okamoto's ringing exhortations struck can be gauged by the responses and echoes long after his most active period. Teshigahara still speaks of the need to retain opposites, while his collaborator Takemitsu speaks of tension, irresolution and irreconcilables as essentials in his work. By 1950, Okamoto was ready to announce his "theory of extreme contrasts" in an article titled "The Non-Sense, the Laugh." It was an important injection of Dada paradoxes in a situation in which Okamoto feared the old proclivities for hierarchical arrangements in the artistic world were reappearing. Okamoto, while defending naiveté in art, offered the young a sophisticated way to avoid the scores of ideological pitfalls awaiting them:

> The fact of attributing signification is something idealistic, but to refuse to see all signification is equally so. It is thanks to the resolution of staying with non-sense that the real sense appears . . . It is precisely the absence of all sense that reflects an acute social conscience . . . It is possible that seriousness is not serious and a joke is not merely a joke. Utter nonsense may

have more power to change social reality than seriousness. What we call the serious joke may the the foundation of art.[7]

For Teshigahara, it was Okamoto's message of discordance, dissonance, and the possibilities inherent in non-sense that hit home while he was still a student. Shortly after he graduated, Okamoto's ideas concerning the most ancient Japanese traditions, which he pointedly represented as superior to the traditions of bygone eras, alerted Teshigahara to the existence of indigenous prehistoric art. Okamoto's expertise, gained in his anthropological studies in Paris, lent him authority when he spoke enthusiastically of a viable aesthetic tradition available in the art of the Jōmon period. He described to his followers the ancient animistic practices that were then being haltingly revealed by archaeologists who, during the 1950s, were examining ancient tumuli and urged them to look attentively at the earliest artifacts produced in Japan.

Okamoto often collaborated with another important figure in the reconstruction of the art world after the war, Kiyoteru Hanada (1909–74). Although Hanada had not been abroad before the war, his knowledge of the avant-garde modernist movements all over the world was, according to Segi, encyclopedic. In general, he entertained a reputation as a man of great integrity, and it was thought that he had resisted the military authorities during the war (although unfriendly critics such as Takaaki Yoshimoto accuse him of joining the Organization for the Reorganization of Culture which professed what Yoshimoto called a kind of Western fascism). Hariu, however, considers him one of the most important figures in the postwar period, comparing his status to that of Walter Benjamin in postwar Europe and crediting him with ushering in the strongest works of the new literary generation in his capacity as general editor of the collection known as *Après Guerre Créatrice*.

Shortly after Hanada had collaborated with Okamoto in founding the Yoru no Kai group, Hanada became one of the most eloquent advocates of political action on the part of artists. He kept his eye on quotidian political events—so turbulent and confusing during the American occupation—and insisted that artists be alert to the first disturbances under MacArthur's regime, such as the prohibition of the general strike in 1947 and the violent disputes of the workers for the Toho Film company. When the Korean War commenced and the United Nations troops were quartered in Japan, Hanada warned his young followers that MacArthur's headquarters could no longer be regarded as the great source of democratic reform. In 1950, in fact, MacArthur had instigated what is known in Japan as the Red Purge, paralleling McCarthy's actions in the United States and going so far as to suppress the Communist newspaper. Hanada responded to these foreboding moves by pressing his view that there existed two avant-gardes, the political and the artistic, and that they needed to be merged. By exhorting students to support large scale political action and to rally against colonialism, imperialism, and the American military presence in Japan, Hanada attracted the disaffected youth and strongly influenced important figures such as Kōbō Abe.

The third, and perhaps most significant, figure influential in the restructuring of the Japanese art world was the poet, painter, and art critic Shūzō Takiguchi. He had been closely associated with André Breton and other Surrealist luminaries such as Paul Eluard and Georges Hugnet. In 1931, he had written a passionate manifesto declaring that, "Poetry is not belief. It is not logic. It is action."[8] In 1935, Christian Zervos solicited an article by Takiguchi on the situation of Japanese artists, and he responded in *Cahiers d'Art*: he attacked what he called the degenerate descendants of haiku and *waka* who had pushed to extremes the purely formal aspects of such poetry. "Japanese poetry lives, thus, in a feudal chateau."[9] As for visual artists, he maintained that translations of Breton and of Aragon's *Painting Challenged* (*La Peinture au Défi*) had had a great impact in spite of the difficulties that Surrealist conceptions encounter in Japan "where the sur-natural elements up to the present have been considered from a humanistic angle of non-sense introduced by Anglo-American literature." Takiguchi cautiously refers to the dismal situation in Japan with its military censorship and points out that reactionary elements bitterly combat revolutionary literature. The censors "suppress above all that word revolution" which, he said, was somewhat amusing since many texts appear filled with blank spaces that almost always signify "revolution."

Despite Takiguchi's reference to a "feudal chateau" housing most of Japan's artists, he and other intellectuals in the 1930s looked precisely to old and feudal traditions in order to find precedents for their own positions. Takiguchi, for instance, wrote about the classical haiku in which he claimed to find the "the spirit of surreality." In 1941, he was arrested by the military authorities, suspected of harboring "dangerous thoughts." His detention spared him the suspicion of collaboration after

Jikken Kōbō (Experimental Workshop), 1954. Among the members are Shūzō Takiguchi (front row, far left) and Tōru Takemitsu (front row, fourth from the right).

the war, and he was honored by the postwar generation as a bona fide resistant. Immediately after the war, Takiguchi became an active promoter of avant-garde values in art, and most especially, of values that could be considered either international or universal. A foe of all nationalism, Takiguchi encouraged young artists to explore every aspect of the modern spirit. He was, according to Ichirō Hariu, the one largely responsible for the establishment of the *Jikken Kōbō* (Experimental Workshop) in which Takemitsu was especially active. The group was avowedly interested in multi-disciplinary art forms, and its members would contribute greatly toward the new tendency after the war to work in what the Japanese call cross-genre modes. Takemitsu was deeply indebted to Takiguchi's broad and highly civilized views on art, and above all, by Takiguchi's sensitive examination of the role of silence in both poetry and music. Several of Takemitsu's most important compositions are based on poetry by Takiguchi, such as his early *Distance de Fée*, the title of a Takiguchi poem that begins with the lines:

Beautiful teeth sun behind the trees
Finely shaped ears were between the clouds[10]

While Teshigahara was taking classes in Western oil painting at the university, he was also an indefatigible explorer, seeking out artists in every medium, listening to their discussions, and spending long nights drinking in small bars near the university. One of his classmates, Matazō Kayama, who was enrolled in the Japanese-style painting department, and who had been sent with Teshigahara to work in the student labor forces, recalls their school days, sketching a picture of Teshigahara as a restless, hearty spirit who smoked and drank and taught Kayama to do the same. Kayama says it is difficult to put those years in perspective, so much was happening, including the recruitment of students for radical political parties. He himself, he says, didn't have enough money even to join a party, and also, since he came from Kyoto, was more conservative, "trained in the idea of *giri* (sense of duty)." Teshigahara, in the accounts of his friends, spent his university years largely outside of the studios, but the few remaining paintings of the period indicate that he was a conscientious and talented painter, that he did his apprenticeship as a fledgling painter with dedication, and that he had been formed by teachers who demanded technical accomplishment. The imagery in some of his paintings ranges from a powerful studio portrait of a young girl in ballet slippers, resting in a chair in a cubist-derived space, her legs strongly drawn and emphasized, to a painting perhaps influenced by postwar Italian painting of the neo-realist style, yet tinged with the fantasy of Surrealism, showing a working class couple, their factory depicted in the background. He holds a stone (or potato?), and she holds a crying child and wears peasant dress. This painting of hunger, with clear sympathy for the starving working class, heralds the moves Teshigahara would make shortly after in an active political life in which his artistic energies were to be channeled into the class-conscious struggle being discussed so fervently among his peers.

Teshigahara remembers the years in his early twenties as fraught with troubling questions for him. "What was most important was to be critical of the Japanese situation." Most of his peers among the visual artists were, as he says, influenced artistically by Surrealism and politically by socialism. "We needed to take a hard look at the real world and assess our position." A friend from those early years, the critic and art historian Shin'ichi Segi, sums up the atmosphere in those first few years after the war: "Everyone, old and young, went to an extreme in art and politics in order to forget or detest the past. This is the reason why so many young artists wanted to be avant-garde or to be communists. There were a number who went to both extremes at the same time."

Segi had been a law student at Chūō University, when he first met Teshigahara. Meanwhile, Teshigahara had met Kōbō Abe through Tarō Okamoto in the Tokyo Metropolitan Museum, and Abe had recruited him for a small group of artists interested in what Teshigahara refers to as "cross-field" art. The group was dominated by Abe, a former medical student who was a few years older. Teshigahara remembers Abe in their first years together as a man interested in all the arts and seeking a way to bring them together. The *Seiki no Kai* amounted to a kind of group education. Abe, Teshigahara says, was eminently talented and was an excellent theorist. "A variety of people gathered around him and many active discussions took place." It didn't take long for the group to arrive at the decision to make their views known. They decided to make a publication, but as they were very poor and had no access to printing presses, they went to a wholesale paper shop, bought very cheap paper, and composed a mimeographed magazine in which they published their own work. Teshigahara remembers the high level of enthusiasm that kept these young artists, writers, and composers at work often the whole night—so much so that Abe eventually fell ill.

A glance at these modest mimeographed publications is enough to demonstrate the degree of serious engagement of its authors and their preoccupations in 1950, the year it appeared. The first issue bears a distinctly Surrealist cover design by Teshigahara and a translation of one of Kafka's stories by none other than the militant Kiyoteru Hanada. The third issue carried an essay by Segi on Piet Mondrian (whose works he had only seen in books he ordered from the important New York art book store, Wittenborn and Schultz). For this issue Teshigahara showed his versatility by drawing an excellent linear portrait of Mondrian in a naturalistic style. Issues number 4 and 5 were devoted largely to early fiction by Kōbō Abe, "Magic Chalk" and "Enterprise." For the cover Teshigahara reverted to his quasi-Surrealist idiom, but inside the magazine he included a strong, realistic portrait of Kōbō Abe.

These portraits by Teshigahara in the first few issues of the magazine were conceived in a linear woodcut style, deriving not so much from the great tradition of ukiyo-e as from the European expressionists. In the sixth issue, the poems of Hiroshi Sekine were featured accompanied by two illustrations by Teshigahara in the Surrealist manner, drawing upon the styles of Dali and Ernst. The seventh and last issue is a bell-wether, prophesying a radical turning in the group's interest. It is devoted to a discussion of literary criticism by a Soviet author. Segi did the frontispiece, and probably soon after, distanced himself from the group. By 1950, Hanada's ideas were becoming extremely attractive to his young collaborators, and Kōbō Abe was no longer, it seemed to Segi, "a good sweet man fond of Rilke whose first poems were romantic." He had now asserted his interest in political action, and even the kind of action that Segi shrunk from—violent protest. From 1950, according to Segi, both Teshigahara and Abe were shedding their previous commitment to Surrealism, and the password, as Segi calls it, would be "sub-realism."

Segi's assessment of that year of collaboration matches Teshigahara's own. It was of crucial importance in his development. With Okamoto's exhortations ringing in his ears—the insistence that his young followers confront the tensions of life, and dare to face ugliness as well as beauty—Teshigahara eagerly followed Abe's lead, reading Western books ranging from Jean Paul Sartre to Kafka, and attending events that brought news from the West in the form of exhibitions and above all, movies. Teshigahara always says that the films brought into Japan soon after the war, particularly the neo-realist films from Italy and France, showed him and others of his generation that resistance had existed in Europe even under the cruel oppression of the Nazis, and that its relative absence in Japan was a serious problem. His entire circle of artistic colleagues was alert to the vestiges of the old imperialist regime and outraged when MacArthur brought Cold War strictures to bear in Japan. "There was certainly an anti-imperialist atmosphere among us then," Teshigahara says. "Japanese politics was out-and-out pro-United States. None of the Japanese politicians were independent, always at the beck and call of the Americans. But Japanese-American relationships had started in a totally colonialistic way, and we couldn't help being critical at that time."

The leftward turning of so many artists around 1950, the year Teshigahara graduated, and the numerous competing ideologies, splits and apostasies made it very difficult for a visual artist, trained academically in the modern tradition, to find a comfortable outlet for his creative energies. Teshigahara and Abe, along with most of the others in his group, threw themselves into a movement advocated by Hanada and Okamoto. The two leaders had prepared them for the upsurge of action during the events of 1950—events that inevitably strengthened the will of young artists to rebel. They were exasperated when they saw the reforms initiated during the Occupation slowly rescinded for reasons, they thought, that had only to do with the American prosecution of the war in Korea. The anti-war movement that swept through Japan's cultural life more than once was initially a general uprising based on the perception that the government was edging toward the restoration of certain unacceptable military positions. Many Japanese citizens were aware of the immense importance of Article 9 in the postwar constitution that renounced war forever and declared "the right of belligerency of the state will not be recognized." The American onslaught in Korea, they felt, compromised the important tenets of the new constitution, and above all, Article 9. University youths rallied to its defense, as they would again during the war in Vietnam when *Beheiren*, an informal, nonaffiliated group supported by Okamoto, once again reminded Japan of its commitment to peace and the necessity of abandoning imperial goals.[11]

Cultural critics documenting the period, whether speaking from the right or left, always underline the importance of political events in the formation of countless, always shifting art groups during the first postwar decade. When the Occupation authorities collaborated with the government in suppressing protest, students organized large demonstrations. Some of them participated in the 1949 protest over the layoffs of railway workers, which was brutally put down. Soon after, there was a conflagration at the Toho film company headquarters so severe that the government brought in tanks. Scenes of the police clubbing strikers inevitably alarmed young intellectuals who immediately associated the brutality with the hated prewar regime.

The situation in postwar Tokyo, as many intellectuals saw it, could be compared to the confusion that reigned in Germany after the First World War, and one of the early manifestos issued by the artist Shunsuke Matsumoto has many points in common with the first manifesto of the German vanguard group, the *Novembergruppe*. Matsumoto had resisted both the military authorities and government-appointed critics during the war. His manifesto, *An Artist's Document*, advocated the establishment of a free and equal artists' union with branches and galleries in the main cities. He advocated free workshops and annual open exhibitions, as well as exchanges with artists abroad. His call for collective action was soon expanded by several artists' groups to include direct action in response to the Korean War that began in June 1950. They opposed the pact between the United States and Japan signed in San Francisco in 1951, which guaranteed the Americans a military base in Japan. Hanada's insistence that artists should function in both political and artistic vanguards was forceful and, around 1950, the idea that artists would go to the people as once Russian revolutionary artists—the nineteenth-century Wanderers and the *Narodniki*—had, began to appeal to more and more youths, even those in Teshigahara's circle who had begun more as aesthetes. Neither Kōbō Abe nor Teshigahara could accept social realism on the Soviet model, but they were casting about for a means that would fuse their artistic interests with their civic indignation. Soon after the San Francisco Treaty, Teshigahara and a dozen other artists and writers took to the mountains where they would experiment with their new "documentary" approach to art.

Among Teshigahara's comrades in the mountains was the filmmaker, Noriaki Tsuchimoto, who vividly remembers their experience. Tsuchimoto had begun his studies at Waseda University as a law student, but by his own account, he spent most of his time at demonstrations and in feverish activities with the student movement. Like others of his generation he had had what he calls "a completely military education" but after the war had joined the Communist Party. In Waseda, he points out, the party was already divided into two factions: those who favored international policies, and those who wanted a strictly national policy.

Tsuchimoto was among the students dispatched to a mountain village to protest the construction of a dam, "even though we knew the villagers were not against it." It was regarded by the leaders in the party "as training to connect with the masses (*taishū*) and we were expected to write articles and make printed leaflets." Teshigahara's account, like Tsuchimoto's, is recounted with some amusement, suggesting that the entire group of city youths was hardly prepared for the task and somewhat naïve. In addition to the Waseda University contingent, there were seven visual artists. "Laborers were already at work at the site," Teshigahara recalls, "and they had been forced to accept extremely severe conditions. Their housing was miserable. We thought it was important for us to get working people to realize how exploited they were." His job was to observe working conditions and to make woodcuts or stencils for printed broadsides and pamphlets. The adventure lasted only a few weeks but was exciting for the city boys who, as Teshigahara laughingly reports, slept under a big boulder and called their arrangement "*sashimi* sleeping."

The goal of inspiring a strike was, of course, not met. But the experience was important to Teshigahara who, as Donald Richie says, came from the "cultural nobility" and had had little contact with the working poor. It could not have been easy for Teshigahara to take to the mountains. He was often perceived by his fellow rebels as a *botchan*, a nice, rich boy to whom you went with your problems (usually economic) and who could be counted on. He was, and to some degree still is, a victim of a kind of reverse snobbery that condemned bourgeois culture and was wary of artists who had had the bad luck to have come from the bourgeoisie.

Yet despite his family's affluence, Teshigahara was at the time living at the same difficult level as his comrades. The young Isozaki, who had come to Tokyo to the university in 1950, at the age of 18, remembers being taken to a very small house with three names on the gate, Jun Ishikawa, Teppei Kataoka, and Hiroshi Teshigahara, who was then living with Kataoka's daughter. Living conditions were extremely harsh, he says, adding that in addition to the three families crammed into minimal space, there were always three or four artists from Teshigahara's art school hanging around. It is of interest that the young Teshigahara was sharing life with an older writer, Jun Ishikawa, who had been an expert on French literature before the war, had translated Gide, was interested in Surrealist automatism, and was a writer of highly experimental prose. At the same time, Teshigahara was seeing Kōbō Abe, and Isozaki recalls Abe's strong theories on art and his particular interest at the time in Picasso, which he believes influenced Teshigahara who, three years younger than Abe, was still a student.

Among various difficulties for Teshigahara was having a father like Sōfū. He could not properly rebel since Sōfū's robust individualism was still very evident. Therefore, the young Teshigahara had to find some territory of his own. With an omni-artistic sire like Sōfū, that was not easy. Teshigahara's turn toward filmmaking might in part have been because it was the one art form Sōfū had not engaged in. Both he and Abe were greatly aroused by the films from Europe and America that they were finally able to see after the war, among them films by the new generation that struck Japanese viewers, inured to war propaganda films for years, with awe. Teshigahara's first encounter with works by Roberto Rossellini, Vittorio de Sica, René Clément, and Luis Buñuel made a huge impression, not only because neo-realism showed him a way out of an artistic dilemma, but because the film technique indicated a way for him to project himself as an artist of conscious commitment without falling into the banality of social realism.

NOTES

1 Andrew E. Barshay, *State and Intellectual in Japan*, Berkeley, 1991, p. 238.

2 Noriko Ohtake, *Creative Sources for the Music of Toru Takemitsu*, Harts, England, 1993, p. 1.

3 Ibid., p. 12.

4 *Reconstructions: Avant-Garde Art in Japan, 1945–1965*, Museum of Modern Art, Oxford, p. 14.

5 Ibid., p. 15.

6 Vera Linhartova, *Dada et Surréalisme au Japon*, Paris, 1987.

7 Tarō Okamoto, *The Non-Sense, The Laugh*, Atelier, Nov. 1950, in *Japon des Avant Gardes*, Paris, 1986, p. 245.

8 Shūzō Takiguchi in *Japon des Avant Gardes*, p. 163.

9 *Cahiers d'Art*, Vol. 5 & 6, 1935.

10 Ohtake, *Creative Sources*.

11 Thomas R. H. Havens, *Fire Across the Sea*, Princeton, 1987, p. 56.

3

*I*n the meetings of the *Seiki no Kai* there were animated discussions of each new exhibition, book, or film coming from the great world that had been closed off by the prewar authorities. Many young artists were in a constant state of excitement. The swift florescence of aggressively avant-garde groups that constantly dissolved and reformed, and in which loyalties were often challenged as they were in political groups, kept Teshigahara and his friends in an exceptional state of receptivity. Not only were forbidden books available now, but a number of exhibitions were brought in from abroad to sharpen their appetites. Various artistic currents in Europe and the United States were conscientiously documented in exhibitions sponsored by large newspapers. In 1950, for instance, *Yomiuri* brought in an exhibition of modern art which included a selection from the Parisian Salon de Mai, and in 1951, they not only brought the first full-scale exhibition of Matisse to Japan, but also included in the third of its Salon des Indépendants a selection of American works by artists who were just becoming celebrated in their own country—Bradley Walker Tomlin, Ad Reinhardt, Jackson Pollock, Mark Tobey, Theodoros Stamos, Clyfford Still, and Mark Rothko, as well as works by internationally known artists such as Wifredo Lam, René Magritte, Jean Dubuffet, and Yves Tanguy. Many young painters were inspired by this exposure to world art and lost no time adopting new vocabularies in their work.

The artists in Teshigahara's circle, however, were reluctant to take up what they considered the traditional art for art's sake stance present even in the most radical idioms of postwar painting. The pull of political commitment impeded them. Teshigahara himself was still hesitating about which direction he should take when he was offered a chance to make a film on the great Japanese artist Hokusai (1760–1849). Although he had already discovered his passion for films, Teshigahara had very little knowledge about how they were made. But with characteristic bravura he threw himself into the project. It was the first of his many considerations of historic figures who could be interpreted as eccentric, or nonconformist, and whose views and tastes were not bound by the physical boundaries of Japan. Working frantically, Teshigahara probed the life of the great draftsman and woodcut artist, which he came to see as a series of radical departures from the consensual nature of Japanese society. He filmed Hokusai's various reflections on the life and culture of his time in sharp black and white, with strong pauses and stop-motion effects to suggest Hokusai's quick intelligence. With notable concision Teshigahara set his theme by offering historic background in a series of maps and period views of the busy streets of nineteenth century Tokyo. He peoples the city with Hokusai's many characterizations of professionals such as Kabuki actors, barrel makers, artists, woodcutters, courtesans, and theatergoers offered in dramatic sequences to form a cultural history of the city. Interspersed among these vivid Hokusai images are shots of real hands cutting into the woodblocks—the first of many close-ups of human hands at work—and still more scenes of citizens of Tokyo at work. Moving out from the big city, Teshigahara films the famous views of landscapes, including Mt. Fuji, and Hokusai's frequent allusion to the sea, with people at work in fishing vessels. In his choices, Teshigahara makes a point of Hokusai's awareness of Western art and his studies of Western perspective, stating his own view, for the first time, that Hokusai's art was never autochthonous. As the film moves toward the denouement, Teshigahara's characterization of Hokusai as finally a solitary artist on a lonely road is emphasized with a voice-over of an actor reading a haiku by Bashō. Throughout the film Teshigahara stresses Hokusai's many displacements, both physical and psychological, and highlights the artist's critique of his society. Hokusai had documented a peasants' rebellion over taxation, for instance, and he had also satirized the life of the warrior class in sardonic drawings that belittle the martial impulse. Teshigahara calls attention to Hokusai's many bankruptcies and his resistance to commercial demands. When his unconventional way of working brought him to the brink of disaster, Hokusai would sell his name to disciples and move on. Hokusai's unusual character and the turnings in his life served Teshigahara both as a means to draw parallels with his own society and to suggest that finally, the visionary artist of great endowments never fits into his culture. He dies, as did Hokusai, an isolated genius.

In finding arresting images in the oeuvre of Hokusai to represent his own feelings, Teshigahara was able to focus the conflicting thoughts that had stirred his own imagination. He was abetted in the difficult formation of a point of view of existence by the strong interest in his group in the new philosophic tendencies in Europe. In 1939, Sartre's *Nausea* had been translated into Japanese, and soon after the war Sartre's other works, and those by fellow Existentialists, became known in Japan. Kōbō Abe was an attentive reader of European journals, moreover, and brought his discoveries to his friends. The respect for the individual, who with acute self-awareness is able to discern the faults in his own thought conventions, was of primary importance to both Abe and Teshigahara in the early 1950s. The whole Existentialist attitude, so steeped in the philosophic issue of authenticity, seemed to them apposite to their own situations. Through having to select and isolate specific motifs in Hokusai's life's work, Teshigahara was able to locate in himself certain strong convictions.

In the course of his work on the Hokusai documentary, Teshigahara met the accomplished documentary film specialist Fumio Kamei, who soon after took him on as an assistant. Kamei had largely learned his métier from an intense study of early Soviet documentary films and dramatic features such as Eisenstein's fictionalized history films. He was such a fanatic enthusiast of the film techniques of Eisenstein, Pudovkin, and Vertov, that in 1928 he went to study at the Leningrad School of Film and Drama. Kamei had worked on feature films for Toho after the war. He was one of the leaders of the striking workers during the notorious strike. When, during the strike, "two thousand Japanese police in steel helmets, American soldiers with automatic weapons, and the commander of the first cavalry in an airplane" attacked the strikers, Kamei was deeply shocked.[1] According to Akira Iwasaki, it became clear to Kamei that above all, Japan needed an independent film movement. He then joined Iwasaki's organization, Shinsei Motion Picture Productions, along with other directors, proposing to produce "democratic pictures with a left-wing flavor."[2]

It was within the new framework that Teshigahara worked as assistant director on three of Kamei's documentary films, learning invaluable lessons in every aspect of filmmaking. Eventually the experience brought him to an understanding of documentary film that he would refine later in his own work. His own limited experience nonetheless stood him in good stead on his first Kamei project: his brief stint in the documentary movement that brought him to the mountains would be helpful in Kamei's film which required that Teshigahara acquaint himself with an authentic grassroots protest movement. The film documented the conflict between villagers and government officials at the Tachikawa air base in Sunagawa. In May 1955, local citizens whose homes adjoined the base protested not only the noise of the American planes, using Tachikawa for air sorties over Korea, but a proposal by the Americans, in collaboration with Japanese defense authorities, to lengthen the runways. The ongoing struggle of the local residents against the powerful military was the subject of Kamei's film. (The battle lasted for years, with a violent demonstration as late as 1967.)

The second film was a documentary about the victims of Hiroshima and Nagasaki. Called ironically, *Life is Wonderful*, Kamei's film forced Teshigahara to consider Kamei's approach carefully, as did the final film he worked on, *The Fears of Humanity*, dedicated to denouncing the use of nuclear weapons. Although he shared Kamei's values, Teshigahara gradually began to question the older artist's approach. He had been persuaded by Okamoto that the artist must hold in suspension both love and hate, outer nature and inner mind, and that he must submit to being torn by these contrasting forces. Okamoto's ideas remained in Teshigahara's thoughts as he watched Kamei soften the blows of truth in the interest of ideology: "Kamei was concerned, perhaps too concerned, with conveying his feelings. Eventually he bypassed contradictions; bypassed brutal truths; the darker side of issues where contradictions enter. Leftists made films to suit their purpose—like bitter medicine covered with something sweet. I found myself more and more alienated. It was too shallow, too ideological."

Teshigahara began to think critically about the nature of the documentary. He was well versed in the neo-realist films of Europe and remembered especially the impact of de Sica's *Bicycle Thief*. To this day he speaks admiringly of the Italian piazzas in sharp light and dark and people moving through. De Sica's tactic of moving all over Rome, never idling in familiar landmarks, and always suggesting a shadowy environment that is almost, but not quite, anonymous, matched Teshigahara's perception of his own city after the war—a city, as his friend Kōbō Abe would describe it in several novels, with no center and a dreadful pervasive vacuity, no matter how quickly the eager builders put up their graceless progeny to make or remake a vanished metropolis. The American filmmaker Martin Scorsese in a tribute to Fellini characterized neo-realism in Italy after the war as a specific and short-lived phenomenon:

> Neo-realism was a moment in world cinema born of historical circumstance (the disastrous conditions of postwar Italy and the limited means of film production), and it became (mostly thanks to Rossellini) a specific style of filmmaking, characterized by the use of real locations, nonprofessional actors, an almost documentary approach to contemporary stories and much technical ingenuity.[3]

It was to be the "almost documentary approach" that Teshigahara eventually embraced, after finding Kamei's methods unsuitable for what he wanted to do. Years later he wrote that his experience with Kamei had taught him one thing: "Documentary films, I soon concluded, are not necessarily the means of recording or reflecting reality. They could be the ideal medium for expressing the director's philosophy as well."[4]

In various interviews over the years, Teshigahara has stressed the importance of the documentary ground in his own films. He told Joan Mellen:

> The real meaning of the documentary film is not the taking of objective shots but that the film has to be interpreted by the director, who feels this way or that and draws some meaning from the subject. You have to add this human element; otherwise the film will not emerge as art. Documentary is the presentation of the subject which is construed and perceived through particular human eyes.[5]

In his own book, published in 1992, Teshigahara stressed the conclusions he came to after leaving Kamei:

This realization came back to me later when I began directing feature films. In making feature films, you of course have to use actors and rely on various techniques that are different from those of the art of making documentary films. But in the basic stance of the director, as I have come to learn, there should be no difference between the arts of making documentaries and feature films.[6]

All of these statements stress the importance of a particular point of view. Teshigahara's intelligence was challenged again and again during that hectic postwar emergence. Previously he had realized the importance of Buñuel's work, and he now began to question Kamei's ideas on the documentary. Buñuel, of course, was a familiar of the leaders of the avant-garde from the older generation. Almost all of them had embraced the Surrealist vision of existence in their youth, and without exception, admired Buñuel. It is not surprising that the master of contrasts should satisfy the aesthetic needs of the youth who had listened to Okamoto and Takiguchi. Teshigahara was impressed by Buñuel's *Los Olvidados*, with its powerful black and white oppositions and strong flow from scene to scene. He liked the way Buñuel positioned people "so that the depths of their minds were hinted at," and the fact that Buñuel never descended to melodrama. Buñuel's films were drawing him away from the ideological direction Kamei represented.

During the 1950s, it was not only Teshigahara's growing interest in the profession of filmmaking that brought him to reconsider the convictions of his student years; as the son of a major figure in the postwar art world, he was constantly exposed to new experiences. Sōfū was one of the active members of a generation energetically engaged in the reconstruction of Japan. He worked closely with the architect Kenzō Tange, and in the mid-1950s, commissioned Tange to build a new building for Sōgetsu complete with an auditorium that could seat 300 people. He would give Hiroshi the chance to orchestrate the new avant-garde tendencies—to bring the youth of Tokyo into contact with major forces from all over the world.

Meanwhile, all through the first years of the 1950s, Tokyo had eagerly welcomed a procession of visitors from the West, almost daily absorbing conflicting points of view and thrashing out differences in the press and many newly-founded art journals. One of the first visitors to stir controversy had been Isamu Noguchi, friend of both Tange and Sōfū. When Noguchi arrived in 1950, there were copious interviews in the press. He quickly met the leading figures in the art world. His message, however, perplexed the youth. Instead of bringing the golden message of Western vanguardism they had expected, Noguchi admonished his listeners to pay attention to their own tradition and not to imitate Western modes that, in his opinion, were already losing momentum. When Noguchi began using local materials such as clay, bamboo, and rope, many young admirers were shocked. They had expected from him the advanced experimental techniques being explored in the West. In addition, they could not understand Noguchi's commitment, which to them seemed too aesthetic. Older colleagues such as Sōfū and Tange, however, understood. Tange, for instance, urged the authorities to employ him on the memorial project in Hiroshima. Noguchi's presence during the 1950s, when he presented his work in the first modern museum in Japan in Kamakura, and when he designed the bridges for Hiroshima and the memorial to his Japanese father at Keiō University, was often resisted by the young. Sometimes, as in the case of Teshigahara, his influence would only be felt years later.

Far more startling to the new generation was the appearance of artists of their own generation from Europe and America. In 1957, for instance, the French promoter of what was known as "informalism," Michel Tapié, arrived in Japan together with Sam Francis, the Japanese artist Toshimitsu Imai, who had been living in Paris, and Georges Mathieu. Tapié had been zealously promoting an international movement from Paris and had taken to the road in the mid-1950s, seeking artists from all over the world to induct into the movement, artists who could in some way conform to his vision of *"un art autre."* In Japan, Tapié quickly found an ally in Sōfū Teshigahara, whose baroque sculptures, often composed of gnarled wooden stumps or mosaic on wood, seemed remote from any traditional modernist art. Probably through Hisao Dōmoto, Tapié met the dynamic founder of the *Gutai* group in Osaka, Jirō Yoshihara, whose life as an artist before the war had been steeped in the most radical vanguard traditions, and who stimulated the young artists in Osaka to seek their expression with the freedom of the original Dada artists. In Tokyo, Tapié was an active gadfly, bringing his theory of informal art to groups of younger artists and speaking frequently to the art press.

His flamboyant companion from Paris, Georges Mathieu, helped to capture the attention of a broad spectrum of viewers when he performed one of his extravagant action paintings in a department store window. Sōfū was so delighted with Mathieu that he acquired a huge painting for his own collection. After the first impact, however, the young Japanese would be somewhat less enthusiastic about Mathieu, whose views on Japan were very much like those of Noguchi. Mathieu's idea of Japan was apparent when he wrote of his sojourn (during which he made twenty-one canvases in three days, one of them on a street location which took up fifteen meters) that he found Japan "the most refined country in the world."[7] In Japan, he said, everything is ordered by art, even the way Japanese dispose four shrimp on a plate, and he concluded that the West had nothing to teach such people.

During those first animated years of the 1950s, Teshigahara watched, listened, maintained his relationships with politically engaged artists, and kept in touch with work issuing from the Experimental workshop. He struggled to sort out the cacaphonous voices of an increasingly diversified artistic culture. The new Sōgetsu building spurred his ambition to bring them all together. When, in June 1958, the new building was inaugurated, he made ambitious plans for its purple-brick hall. Yet, in his own work he felt increasingly frustrated. He "sensed the emptiness of the ideological activities of the artists" but had still not found a path out of the wilderness of arguments raging in art circles in Tokyo. When his father asked him to accompany him to America, where Tapié had arranged an exhibition of Sōfū's sculptures, and then to Europe, Teshigahara more than willingly accepted.

NOTES

1   Joseph Anderson and Donald Richie, *The Japanese Film: Art and Industry*, New York, 1960, p. 238.

2   Ibid., p. 238.

3   Martin Scorsese, "Amid Clowns and Brutes, Fellini Found the Divine," *The New York Times*, Oct. 24, 1993, p. H21.

4   Hiroshi Teshigahara, *Furuta Oribe*, NHK Press, Tokyo, 1992.

5   Joan Mellen, *Voices from the Japanese Cinema*, New York, 1975, p. 171.

6   Teshigahara, *Furuta Oribe*.

7   Georges Mathieu, in *Japon des Avant Gardes*, p. 273.

4

When he thinks back to the late 1950s and his personal dilemma as an artist, Teshigahara says, "I was like a frog at the bottom of a dry well, with fog in his mind." His first trip abroad in 1959 proved to be a watershed in his life. "The impact of that trip blew the fog right out of my system." The first stop for Sōfū's entourage (the *iemoto* travelled with assistants and family, all of whom were engaged in the mounting of his exhibitions) was New York. Teshigahara waxes enthusiastic when he speaks of his first impressions. He remembers New York as a very clean city in which the people looked rich and satisfied. In the course of helping his father to install his exhibition at the Martha Jackson Gallery, Teshigahara met many artists who dropped into the gallery, saw Jackson's collection, which included several works by Jackson Pollock, and was invited to various nightspots with people in Jackson's circle. For Teshigahara, meeting artists who were not embroiled in the ideological arguments he had left behind in Tokyo was extremely refreshing. For the first time he could imagine a community of artists working freely, unencumbered by the moral issues that so much bedeviled his own. There was a whirlwind of visits: touring the city on foot; going to the most celebrated jazz hangout, the Five Spot, which was thronged with painters, to hear Charles Mingus; and attending a party given by Norman Mailer in his Brooklyn apartment. Some of the time he was accompanied by the photographer Ishimoto, who had been trained at the Chicago Bauhaus.

During these weeks, Teshigahara reviewed his past. "Before leaving

Japan, I'd had conflicts with friends and former colleagues. Abroad I realized how shortsighted the scope of Japan was, with the endless conversations about revolutions and the role the artist played in them. In New York, the revolution was constantly going on." One day, Teshigahara was introduced to the sports photographer Marvin Newman, who told him about a 22-year old Puerto Rican boxer, José Torres. Teshigahara went with Newman to the boxer's gym and, as he says, it was a case of love at first sight. "Torres was a fantastic boxer." Teshigahara immediately went to a local camera shop, borrowed a 16 millimeter camera to supplement the camera he already had, and returned to the gym to record his impressions of the training. This lasted two days and on the third, he witnessed Torres' tenth professional fight, filming from the ringside. Part I of the film *José Torres*, a 25-minute documentary, inaugurated a new epoch for Teshigahara. Like many filmmakers in the United States, he honored the idea of the hand-held camera and the home movie look. Experimental filmmakers in the United States were in full rebellion against the technique-oriented slickness of commercial film, and the artless style was much appreciated. At the same time, the rebellion among artists Hiroshi's age in New York against the high seriousness of the older painters of the New York School was taking shape in the form of a simplified, and sometimes artless, art that quickly became known as "pop art."

Perhaps Teshigahara's choice of José Torres as a subject was influenced by the American tides. Perhaps his choice of a man of the people was a way to assuage his social conscience. In any case, it was far from the subject matter of most Japanese films of the time, and in its deliberate roughness and unedited quality, was something of a manifesto. Teshigahara's scenes of the dilapidated streets near Torres' gym, of the denizens of the fight world, and of the drama and suspense attending the preparation for a big fight are registered with a fine sense of rhythm, one of his distinguishing characteristics. The mounting tensions are very sparely inflected by Tōru Takemitsu's score and sound effects—the first of many for Teshigahara's films. When old friends recall Teshigahara's work as a film director, they inevitably return to *José Torres*, which made a strong impression when he showed the first part only months after he returned to Japan.

From New York, the Teshigahara entourage moved on to Europe, which would provide the young filmmaker with yet another important

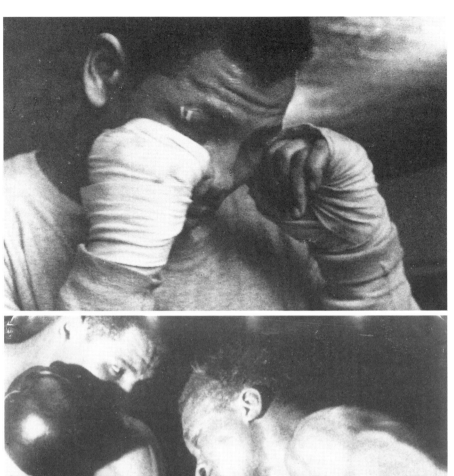

Scenes from Teshigahara's documentary film José Torres *(1959).*

experience of self-discovery, although not nearly as intense as the shock of New York. Europe had been far more accessible to young Japanese artists. Most of the older artists they could respect had been formed by experiences in Europe, and particularly in prewar Paris. New York, as Teshigahara says, was for him the apex of the twentieth century, while

Paris was almost familiar to him, having wandered in his father's art books for so many years. The group arrived shortly after André Malraux had swept through the city cleaning the old buildings, bringing them back to their original light colors. Teshigahara breathed in the atmosphere of the eighteenth and nineteenth centuries as he strolled around Paris.

When Sōfū's show opened at the Galerie Stadler, many artists came and responded with enthusiasm. To some degree, the Teshigahara event was of importance to many French artists who themselves were looking for other sources of inspiration. The firm figure of the aged flower-arranger, so sure of his position, and representing an old tradition that he had managed to renew, was attractive. Some of the Japanese artists who had paved the way, such as Hisao Dōmoto, who had installed himself in Paris in 1955, and Toshimitsu Imai, met with Hiroshi Teshigahara. Their conversation was spirited, comparing the free atmosphere of Paris with the atmosphere in Tokyo that they perceived as restricting and hopelessly mired in rhetoric.

There were other memorable events during that important voyage. Hiroshi was in a preternaturally receptive mood and would draw upon his impressions for many years to come. For instance, during a trip to Italy, Sōfū was invited to participate in an international exhibition in Torino. After installing his sculptural works, Sōfū made a huge calligraphic painting for the back wall of his installation that his son would never forget. Perhaps the most significant impression Teshigahara registered during that fateful trip occurred when Tapié took them sightseeing in Spain. One of their first visits was to Salvador Dalí, who was then living in a fisherman's house in Porto Ligato. Dalí had once entertained great popularity in prewar Japan. Both Teshigaharas were eager to meet the great Surrealist master. When they arrived, Dalí greeted them wearing a *yukata* and a scarlet rose in his ear to honor the Japanese flower arranger. Sōfū was so moved that he wanted to reciprocate. He made an ikebana for the Surrealist master from driftwood and a lacquerware bowl.

Meeting Dalí was a pleasant diversion, but the most important encounter for Teshigahara was with the unique work of the master-builder, Antonio Gaudí, which as he reports, left him totally astonished, stunned, overwhelmed. When he first glimpsed Casa Millá, he felt that he had finally found an answer to his long years of questioning the

Salvador Dalí at his home in Porto Ligato in 1959, posing for Hiroshi Teshigahara.

artificial boundaries in the arts. "His works made me realize that the lines between the arts are insignificant . . . that the world in which I was living still left a great many possibilities." Almost immediately he began to document the works of Gaudí in Barcelona and its environs, using a camera to scale the sculptured and mosaic-laden walls and to catch the amazing sweep of Gaudí's multimedia genius. This sequence of 16 millimeter film remained with him for years. Eventually, Teshigahara returned to Barcelona to complete his undertaking in a meticulously detailed, sober survey of Gaudí's life's work.

The deluge of impressions of places, artistic life, popular mores, landscapes and individual artists changed Teshigahara's view of his own life. "In my mind, everything was shining. I had found a firm ground."

Photographs taken by Hiroshi Teshigahara of Antonio Gaudí's Parque Güell (left) and Sagrada Familia (below) in Barcelona.

When he returned to Japan he was brimming with ideas about projects, among them his films on Torres and Gaudí, but also ideas about how to use Sōgetsu Hall. "After so many difficulties with ideology, it was natural that I would take the plunge into creative activities that knew no bounds. I came back to Tokyo with a deep urge to touch off an artistic movement. Before the war, there had been the seeds of growth but imperialism had wiped them out—those seeds did not bear fruit. The artistic movement I wanted to initiate had no parallel." He wanted to "provide an arena where artists themselves would be the producers of activities." Teshigahara's idea was that individuals from all fields of art would come together voluntarily and create new forms. He was in a perfect position to carry out his vision. He had control of the hall at Sōgetsu, was well known among artists in various positions and fields, had a personality that was conciliatory and generally open, and already knew something about working collaboratively since the very nature of his primary art, filmmaking, required it. Moreover, his early experiences with fellow artists in experimental groups, such as Jikken Kōbō, had already predisposed him to the idea that all the arts should be brought together if new forms were to invigorate Japanese art. The lessons of Okamoto and Hanada had been fruitful. Ever since the mid-1950s, energetic groups had been working in what was called cross-genre art. Several of Teshigahara's old friends were ready to collaborate with him on the creation of a movement whose nucleus would be Sōgetsu Art Center.

A cursory glance at the programs that took place at the Center during the first few years after Teshigahara's return from Europe indicates the extent to which the idea of an art without boundaries was explored. Nearly every art was honored in its activities, and often several simultaneously. In addition to performances of a most extravagant kind, there were educational evenings in which Teshigahara introduced films from abroad, or discussions of recent events or art forms of the past, such as American jazz that had influenced modern art. Certain artists who would soon deposit important vanguard art forms in modern art history in Japan had their first works performed at Sōgetsu, and others, already working in Tokyo, undertook their most adventurous programs there. Yoshiaki Tōno, one of Japan's most lively critics of the period, called the Sōgetsu Art Center "the epicenter of the avant-garde." Teshigahara's old friends rallied to the call. Takemitsu, for instance, performed in April 1960, his *musique concret* experiment *Water Music*. This is a montage of natural sounds of water based on Takemitsu's images of different states of water, ranging from mud puddles to a drop on a leaf. For this occasion, one of Teshigahara's oldest friends, the Noh actor Hideo Kanze, was enlisted to dance which, as the critic Kuniharu Akiyama points out, was not so strange since the amplified sounds of dripping water came through like a Noh drum.

The burgeoning movement in modern dance found a home in Sōgetsu, and some of the most extravagant and innovative techniques were first presented there. Japan had long before had a brief moment of exuberant dance experimentation when, immediately after the 1923 earthquake, groups such as *Mavo* and *Sanka* staged riotous performances using the talents not only of dancers, but painters and sculptors as well. Several artists associated with these groups had been abroad, and those who had been in Germany had been inspired by the work of modern pioneers such as Mary Wigman and Harold Kreuzberg.

One of them, Tomoyoshi Murayama (1901–1977), was an exceptionally active participant in the rich variety of artistic activity he encountered during a sojourn of less than a year in Berlin, from February 1922 to January 1923. Experiencing the full panoply of artistic experimentation, ranging from Dada performances involving artists, poets, and actors, as well as unorthodox composers, to the experimental theater of Expressionists such as Georg Kaiser, Murayama was fired with an ambition to instigate events in Japan encompassing all the arts. His own talent as a painter was extended to dance, which he hoped to transform just as he hoped to transform painting and sculpture, with a dynamic concept of fusion. In an article of 1923, Murayama explained that he had dedicated his exhibition in May 1923, "to over-bearing beauty, because I hate the present Frenchified, overly-calm, self-centered, death-like, degenerate condition of Japanese art."[1] With an eruptive effusion of events, much like later "happenings," Murayama organized a one-day manifestation in June 1924, that did indeed stir things up, if only for a short time. In his *Theatrical Autobiography* (1974), he described:

> The smell of grilled fish, the roar of motorcycles, absurd theater in which the spectators could not hear the actors; a group of workers surging forward and breaking a cinema screen; then a monkey in its cage, and a prostitute who plants herself

there and gives birth. Murayama presents himself with a shaved head and improvised dance without music.[2]

In other performances, Murayama presented himself with a Dutch-boy haircut. His active interest in dance is attested to in a photograph of the year 1924 taken in his studio. Three members of the *Mavo* group are shown in acrobatic poses, one of them suspended upside down, prefiguring the many contorted positions invented by groups associated with the Butoh movement after 1960. The critic Aomi Okabe, writing of Murayama's leading ideas, called it "an aesthetic of chaos and deformation."[3]

This short-lived modern dance movement was only vaguely known to the postwar generation, but there is some reason to believe it nonetheless affected the young through the presence of Kazuo Ōno (1906–   ) to whom Tatsumi Hijikata (1928–1986) deferred. Ōno was old enough to remember the astonishing events of the 1920s and had been marked by the Expressionism of the Germans, passing it along to Hijikata during a twenty-year association with the troupe. Hijikata's profoundly shocking new dance that came to be called by the generic name Butoh, derived from the title of his widely remarked work, *Ankoku Butoh* (Dance of Shadows) of 1961, introduced a note of willful violence in the Sōgetsu programs. Although Teshigahara himself did not relish the extremely tormented style that always assaulted tabus, Butoh was an undeniably original and forceful impulse during the 1960s and paralleled the violent underground American films introduced in the ongoing cinema series at the Center. These artists shared a nihilistic view of life, well expressed in Hijikata's own description of his work: "Butoh is a cadaver which keeps itself standing up with the energy of despair."[4] Donald Richie, in a sensitive essay on Hijikata, recalls an occasion when the two were drinking in a country inn near the sea, overlooking fields where the rice crop was ripening. Hijikata, musing aloud, said:

> That's where it all comes from: the paddy fields . . . you have no idea how tired my parents used to get. They got so tired working in the paddies that they couldn't move, and yet, they had to. It hurt to move. And yet they had to work. No energy, nothing to move with, and yet they moved . . . [5]

Hideo Kanze, who spent a month with Hijikata's troupe and danced with him at Sōgetsu, also sees the origin of Hijikata's dance technique as close to the earth. In Japanese dance tradition in general, Kanze observes, there is a deep connection to the earth, as is well illustrated by the Noh style of walking with the toes up. But unlike Noh dance, Butoh showed a strong tendency to emphasize brutal sexuality, equating eroticism with violence. The nearest relatives to Hijikata's dance were probably the theater of Artaud, with its celebration of cruelty, and the experiments of Grotowsky that were early remarked in Japan.

The new underground theater that sprang up in the wake of the failure to block the treaty in 1960 was also represented at Sōgetsu by some of its most radical proponents. When Teshigahara recalls the high moments during his aegis, he always points to the early works of Shūji Terayama (1935–1983) and Jūrō Kara (1940–   ) performed at Sōgetsu Hall and considered seminal in the alternative theater tradition. Richie, who followed theater developments in the early 1960s attentively, sees

Poster for Jūrō Kara's play John Silver, *staged in May 1967 at Sōgetsu Art Center. Poster design by Tadanori Yokoo.*

parallels in the dance of Hijikata and theater of Terayama, both of whom drew upon the "crudest excesses of prewar melodrama."[6] Terayama's theater draws upon the decor of the Taishō and early Shōwa periods, such as advertisements, uniforms, faded photos, a sword or two and old Japanese flags. He has a predilection for "marginal beings, deformed, and grotesque" and in his expressionist approach "produces a theater for the eyes, not ears." In fact, Terayama, who was inspired by Kabuki traditions, shared with Jūrō Kara a conviction that theater had to be a total art, engaging all the senses and incorporating music, mime, decor, dance, and sound in equal measure. In his essay, "To a Cultural Scandalmonger," Kara wrote:

> If there is anything to the phrase "dramatic imagination" it means the dramatic power that seeks to negate the reality of the spoken word reverberating rhythmically inside each actor.[7]

Both Terayama and Kara mistrusted language, perhaps because both had experienced the way that language had borne aloft the delusions sponsored by the prewar military regime. In an interesting response to Joan Mellen's questioning, Terayama said that he considered himself high on the list of "dangerous thinkers" in Japan. For him, theater was "a crime," as he declared in one of his manifestos in which he said that he and his troupe would "whip the world with our imagination and theatricalize revolution. . . . We as a group will reform the world through poetry and imagination."[8] He exhorted his players to take power with imagination. Terayama specifically sought to eliminate what he referred to as "the artificial frontiers" between drama and reality, and to that end promoted audience participation, destruction of the conventional set, and sometimes the elimination of make-up and costume.

Terayama's ironic references to art as a "crime" were echoed around the same time by the painter Shigeo Ishii in an article titled "The Perfect Crime and Art." As summarized by Kaido Kazu, Ishii claimed that the assassination of the Socialist party leader in 1960, or police actions during the demonstrations, were relatively innocent because they were allowed to surface and were reported in the newspapers.[9] But the perfect crime is something against which law and order are ineffective: "The social condition of Japan is now built upon the perfect crime committed by contemporary imperialism . . . a peaceful situation is allowed to continue in order to protect such a perfect crime."[10] The artist, he declared, could only combat the "perfect crime" by cultivating within himself a power equal to that of his opponents. Similarly, Terayama told Mellen that he no longer believed in political revolutions but only sexual revolution. "I believe that crime and the criminal are revolutionary responses."[11] He also assumed an extremist view that played with the notion of "crime" and reversed values in order to challenge received ideas. One of his novels, *Letters from Sagawa*, was severely criticized by Ian Buruma for the way it took a news story and distorted it. "Murder, in Kara's book, is neither analyzed nor condemned but is aestheticized. . . . Morality, or lack of it, is never an issue, neither is playing fast and loose with the truth. The author is judged on his style."[12] Others have seen in the cruel burlesque style of the theater of the 1960s in Japan a searing critique of Japanese society not unlike theater developments elsewhere. They have pointed to works of authors in Europe, who revitalized Artaud's Theater of Cruelty, or the United States, who replenished the forces of expressionist drama—above all, The Living Theater—or to the total theater approach of Grotowsky as parallels. The emphasis on the human body as the locus of all values, and all transgressions, was not limited to theater. The young American filmmakers such as Kenneth Anger, Stan Brakhage, and Jack Smith, whose often outrageous sadomasochistic films were shown in Sōgetsu's avant-garde ongoing film program, shared much with the new Japanese theater people who were seen in Sōgetsu before they made their full and influential statements a few years later.

As a kind of impresario, Teshigahara was constantly present in the hall, and still young, could be swept up in the vast energies the various explosively defiant artists brought to its stage. He watched and responded, selecting elements that he needed for his own work. By temperament he was not easily drawn into the tempestuous and often scandalous ambiance created, for instance, by Hijikata. He found something "very humid, oppressive in a particularly Japanese way" in Hijikata's performances, as well as in the plays of Kara and Terayama. "They were too dark for my taste." On the other hand, he was enthusiastic about the work of the Polish artist and theater director Tadeusz Kantor, "who was also dark, but in a different way." The difference he sensed lay probably in the way Kantor avoided overt representations of the unspeakable atrocities of the Second World War—although they were the fundamental subjects of almost all his performances—and sought, rather, to stimulate the imagination of his viewers through highly symbolic means. As Teshigahara would prove in his own subsequent work, he had an affinity for subtle, psychological effects rather than violent illustrations.

Month by month at this important juncture in his life Teshigahara observed the swelling tide of anarchism and violence gripping Japanese arts. Yet, the oppressive darkness of the new theater was to some degree countered by the openly dadaistic attitudes of other artists, particularly those brought from New York to perform at Sōgetsu. There was, for instance, strong interest in the ideas of John Cage who, long before he came to Tokyo to perform at Sōgetsu, had been known to active young participants in the Experimental Workshop. The composer Toshi Ichiyanagi (1933–) had studied with Cage in the 1950s and helped Teshigahara make arrangements to bring Cage to Japan. In October 1962, Cage arrived with David Tudor for several performances, in one of which he was assisted by one his admirers, Yōko Ono. She herself gave a memorable performance that same year in which she sat at the piano, crossed her arms, and made repeated movements toward the piano. Eventually she started hitting the keys repeatedly with her elbows—an iconoclastic gesture that conventional concert-goers in Tokyo received in a state of outraged shock.

Perhaps Okamoto's remarks on the value of laughter and non-sense affected Teshigahara's response. In general, he seemed far more comfortable with the spirited, and often funny, happenings favored in the New York neo-dada milieu than he did with the earnest and violent antics of his countrymen. After the performances by Cage and the young Japanese visual artists and musicians who instantly rallied to his side, there would be appearances by Jasper Johns, who took part in an evening of "collective music," and by Merce Cunningham, who linked up with students of traditional Japanese dance for an evening of experimentation. In 1964, there were performances of: Jean Genet's *The Maids*; Terayama's important play, *Study of Vampire*; and evenings of concrete poetry. Throughout the life of the Sōgetsu Art Center, from June 1959 to April 1971, there were regular film showings in the section called the Cinemathèque and frequent concerts of vanguard music from all over the world including American jazz. Enthusiastic colleagues, such as the poet and music critic Kuniharu Akiyama, took part in running the

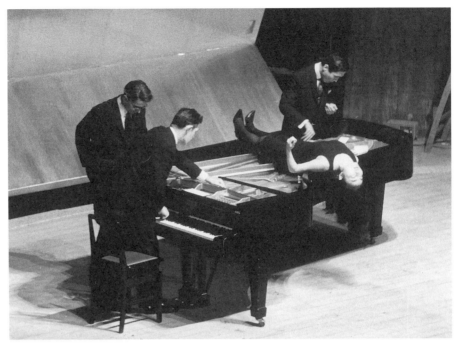

Performance by John Cage at Tokyo Bunka Kaikan in Ueno, October 1962. From left to right: David Tudor, John Cage, Yoko Ono, and Toshirō Mayuzumi.

Scene from performance by Merce Cunningham Dance Company at Tokyo Sankei Hall, November 1964.

hall, while Teshigahara divided his energies between his activities as a filmmaker and his duties as the director of the center. The procession of immensely varied events and the unorthodox character of the performers enabled him to define more specifically the direction his own talents might take and what he wished to avoid. By the early 1960s, Teshigahara was ready to undertake a major project.

NOTES

1   Tsutomu Mizusawa, "Japanese Dada and Constructivism: Aspects of the Early 1920s," in *Dada and Constructivism*, Tokyo, 1988, p. 29.

2   Tomoyoshi Murayama, *Theatrical Autobiography #2*, Tokyo, 1974.

3   Aomi Okabe in *Japon des Avant Gardes*, p. 349.

4   Donald Richie, *Different People*, Tokyo, 1987, p. 98.

5   Ibid., *Different People*, p. 93.

6   Donald Richie, *A Lateral View: On Avant-Garde Theatre*, Berkeley, 1992, p. 137.

7   Jūrō Kara, "To a Cultural Scandalmonger," cited in *Alternative Japanese Drama*, ed. Robert T. Rolf and John K. Gillespie, Honolulu, 1992, p. 256.

8   Shūji Terayama, cited in Mellen, *Voices from the Japanese Cinema*, p. 275.

9   Shigeo Ishii, "The Perfect Crime in Art," cited by Kaido Kazu in *Reconstruction: The Role of the Avant-Garde in Postwar Japan*, Museum of Modern Art, Oxford, 1985.

10 Ishii, *Reconstruction*.

11 Mellen, *Voices from the Japanese Cinema*, p. 216.

12 Ian Buruma, *Behind the Mask*, New York, 1984, p. 223.

5

*A*mong those of Teshigahara's generation who emerged from the war with deeply pessimistic feelings, there was a keen interest in the intellectual news from Paris. Many of them were not comfortable with the old-style Japanese politics, with its emphasis on the imperial system. The humanistic breadth of Existentialism together with its strong emphasis on social commitment offered them an appealing alternative.

The struggle to accommodate the idea of collective action with that of the singular importance of the individual was acute among those in Teshigahara's circle and was in fact a principal motif in the development of Japanese radicalism. Even more, according to Teshigahara's friend, the poet Makoto Ōoka, it was one of the characteristics of the history of Japanese poetry. He speaks of "the continuing interplay, sometimes struggle, between the 'banquet' of communal involvement and the private vision of the 'solitary' mind."[1] In several of his essays, Ōoka stresses the tension between what he calls "the world of the collective spiritual body" and the world of the solitary mind.

Tension, not the much vaunted harmony in Japanese cultural history, was what animated the visions of Teshigahara and his colleagues. They educated themselves in the same sources that had nurtured Sartre—Kierkegaard, Dostoyevsky, and Nietszche above all—and sought confirmations of their own intuitions. Sartre's novel, *Nausea*, enjoyed a revival all over the world during the 1950s. For readers such as Ōoka, it was of importance, especially when they noted that before Sartre accepted the final title from his publisher, Gaston Gallimard, he had used as a working title, *Essay: On the Loneliness of the Mind*. Sartre's work was widely discussed in Japanese literary journals, and most particularly his short story about contingency and death during the Spanish Civil War, "The Wall." Its somber message was easily assimilated by the generation that had experienced, while adolescents, the contingencies attendant on their own war.

By the end of the 1950s, the thoughts that had been gradually cohering in Teshigahara's mind, including thoughts about Buñuel's social message, about Existentialism as a viable philosophy, and about Okamoto's provocative contentions, began to goad him into seeking his own expressive voice. After completing the editing of *José Torres*, he was determined to undertake a full-length feature film and began seeking a suitable scenario. By chance, he saw a television documentary with a script by Kōbō Abe and made a decision to renew his collaboration with his old friend.

By this time, Abe had produced film scripts of considerable importance in Japanese film history. In 1953, he had written the screenplay for Masaki Kobayashi's controversial film, *The Thick-Walled Room*. This film was based on the journals of lesser war criminals who, in Kobayashi's view, had been "victims of the system itself, first because they had to obey the orders of their superiors while the war was going on, and second because they were punished after the war for performing their 'duty.'"[2] The film was deemed so inflammatory by the authorities that its release was postponed for four years. Kobayashi's uncompromising attitude toward the military and his existentialist pacifist views would later be highly praised when he made his epic anti-war film, *The Human Condition*.

Abe, whose intelligence and imagination had governed his sorties into world literature and current events, was still in the existentialist parlance an *engagé* artist, who frequently posed for himself the issues that most attracted Teshigahara: human loneliness and the longing for solidarity. Teshigahara had followed Abe's work attentively, and his collaborations with Abe resulted in four films. Abe's influence, which the younger Teshigahara had experienced as a raw youth, was significant in his coming of age as an artist in film.

In the late 1940s, Abe's aesthetics were decidedly grounded in his political convictions. The architect Isozaki remembers Abe's forceful

Hiroshi Teshigahara with Kōbō Abe.

talks about Picasso, and in general the strong, even hectoring role he played among his younger associates. Others remember a tender romantic who loved the poetry of Rilke. Teshigahara, who made his way amongst the various contentious voices during the 1950s, was strongly drawn to Abe not only because of the older man's firm political stance but because his own intuitions as a visual artist were often confirmed in Abe's literary works. Despite his theory of reportage, Abe's literary inspiration was drawn initially from authors for whom the element of fantasy was marked. It was natural for Teshigahara, whose most exalted model was the film artist Buñuel, to seek in Abe's works a source of inspiration. Abe's presence in his life as a creative kindred spirit cannot be underestimated. The fundamental view of the world they propounded together remained an underlying preoccupation in Teshigahara's later undertakings.

Teshigahara's growth as an artist was always marked by his encounters with others and frequent collaborative exchanges. With Abe, his experience had begun with the magazine where several of Abe's early stories appeared. The author's early work—mostly short stories—provided him, to an unusual degree, with workbooks for his major novels of the 1960s. In the stories, many of the motifs of later works are sketched, and many of the voices of his personal literary culture can be detected. Abe was most evidently inspired by Kafka, but there were other indications of whom he had visited in literature. The forlornness of Kafka's individual confronted by a baffling, labyrinthine existence had been anticipated in Japanese literature by Natsume Sōseki who, in the novel *Kokoro*, had written: "You see, the loneliness is the price we have to pay for being born in this modern age, so full of freedom, independence, and our own egotistical selves."[3]

Abe's frequent characterization of divided selves—characters who lose their identity, have incidents of amnesia, or find new identities as nonhumans, also suggests his familiarity with Russian literature with its long traditions of doppelgänger stories, ranging from Gogol to Dostoyevsky (especially the latter's "The Double"), and to Mandelstam in the twentieth century. As a passionate radical, Abe followed the paths of the early martyrs in Japan's first twentieth-century radical movement who had steeped themselves in Russian literature, some of it frankly offering social critique, but some, such as Gogol's "Dead Souls," offering grander and more universal visions. Abe shared the muted satirical impulse Gogol so deftly controlled, and sometimes made oblique allusion to the Russian master, as in his 1953 play, *The Ghost Is Here*, where the protagonist cunningly swindles a community with a scheme to buy photographs of dead individuals.

There are many allusions in Abe's early stories to both Japanese and Western classics. Like his literary peers, Abe had resolutely turned away from the psychologism of the "I"-novel, which he shunned as bourgeois sentimentalism, but he was unwilling to bend to the demands of social realism, as did some of his comrades in the documentary movement. His early association with prewar Surrealists had freed him from doctrinaire approaches and, by the end of the 1940s, he permitted his imagination to roam freely, incorporating both the grotesque and the fantastic, the earthy—reminiscent of Bertolt Brecht's treatment of beggars in the *The Threepenny Opera*—and the preternatural. Certain images that insistently appear in his oeuvre are well grounded in literary tradition but are heightened and given twentieth-century connotations. The mirror, for instance: There is the ancient origin myth of Japan in which the mirror plays a crucial role in the story of the sun goddess, Amaterasu. The myth is kept kept alive by Shintō priests who, to this day, bring out the mirror, symbolizing the gods, during certain festivals. The ghostly reflection in the mirror, the strangeness, and the self-estrangement of mirror views are obsessive motifs in Abe. Often his characters catch glimpses of themselves in cafe windows or the glass of telephone booths and are as startled and disturbed as Sartre's Roquentin, who approaches his visage in the mirror closely enough to touch it. His eyes, his nose, and his mouth disappear, Sartre writes, and there is nothing human left, only crevasses, molehills. Yet, in spite of everything, "this lunar world is familiar to him."

Although Abe never permitted his earliest stories to be reprinted, one of his works in which was trying his Icarus-like wings with extravagant fantasy appeared in his collected works. In the 1949 story, "Dendrocacalia," the main character, instead of turning into an insect as in Kafka's *Metamorphosis*, turns into a plant, but not before the author indulges in a longish discussion of Dante's *Canto XIII* and a scholarly survey of all Greek myths in which humans are punished by being turned into plants.

By 1951, when he published *The Wall* to great acclaim, Abe had eliminated obvious literary references (although the title might suggest Sartre's presence). In the story, "The Crime of S. Karma," the hero, called K., strongly suggests Kafka's shadowy presence and is even, like Kafka's K., an insurance employee. In this story Abe proposed a theme he would later explore exhaustively: the loss of memory, which is to say, identity. There are still Gogolian overtones, as in the line, "My name had gotten up and left of its own volition," which in later works Abe would eliminate.

Abe's critical attitude toward the politics of the postwar period, dominated by the Occupation authorities, appears in another story of 1951, "Intruders," in which he mocks the parody of democracy he felt had developed in Japan by depicting the intruders, who grab K's money and squat in his modest apartment and enslave him, while as "democrats" they chant slogans such as "Time is Money," "Democracy is Based on Humanism," and "You mustn't spare any efforts for the common welfare of all." In 1954, Abe took on the issue of Japan's aggression during the long war and the misfortune of ordinary people, writing one of his most powerful ghost stories, "Record of a Transformation," in which common soldiers are brutally murdered by their officers, as implied by the Kobayashi film he had collaborated on around the same time.

By 1960, Abe had mastered his means, balancing allegorical and realistic elements with ingenuity. His social critique continued in such stories as "The Bet," in which he recast the Robinson Crusoe story as a fable of "the monstrosity we call modern life." Dark humor prevails as he sketches a portrait of a modern architect called upon to devise the impossible by creating two adjoining rooms, but on different floors. By 1960, the futurist vision of modern building had swamped central Tokyo with skyscrapers planted in totally chaotic sequences. In Abe's story, the building becomes a labyrinth in which the architect himself gets lost, wandering amongst employees of a large firm specializing in advertising slogans—employees, as a professor of psychology retained by the firm explains, who have "already entrusted their soul to the system." Such allegorical stories made a great impression, and strong traces of Abe's vision remain among young writers today.

In the fall of 1960, Teshigahara saw Kōbō Abe's television drama, *Purgatory*, based on a coal mine dispute in Kyūshū. He instantly saw possibilities for a black and white feature-length film, and telephoned Abe who readily agreed. The two set out early in December location hunting. Teshigahara's idea "was to match the allegorical plot, typical of Kōbō Abe, against the deteriorated coal mine city as an extremely realistic background." The two artists finally located a desolate abandoned mining town huddling beneath a gigantic slag heap. Abe wrote the film script quickly, and the following summer, Teshigahara embarked on his first, and eventful, shooting of a feature film.

The elaborate experience of organizing a full-scale feature confirmed Teshigahara's conviction that collaboration among artists always offers "fresh potentials and unbounded possibilities." *Pitfall* was, in a way, a manifesto for himself affirming the importance of the documentary style that—as he had been quick to observe in Buñuel—could be put into the service of a subjective expression of political and social situations.

The impact of Buñuel's *Los Olvidados* can be felt in many of Teshigahara's choices of imagery on location. Buñuel had filmed Mexico's street urchins in starkly calculated black and white. He focused his camera frequently on details that expressed his views on poverty and sometimes depravity, eliminating the need for dialogue. Above all, he relied on the sweep of his camera's view to not only set the scene, both indoors and outdoors, but to describe the circumstances governing the miserable lives he reported.

In the making of *Pitfall*, Teshigahara was a zealous and exacting director. Kanze, whom he impressed for the role of a policeman,

TESHIGAHARA'S
LIFE
IN ART

•

87

remembers his "forceful perfectionism"—the fact that he would not let a scene go without achieving a "perfect improvisation." Teshigahara himself retains indelible memories of the difficulties of commanding a team and the attendant mishaps from which he learned a great deal. Since the film was to be a low budget film, he had only eight crew members. "They knew I was shooting my first film and they didn't trust me at all." The very first scene, showing the unemployed miner's child shaping muddy clay, seemed to them pointless. They consistently challenged him and were slow to follow his lead. One day, for instance, he stood outside a dilapidated sweet shop, studying the great slag heap. "I saw some dots moving and I realized that this was a group of dogs left behind—dogs that had turned wild. Suddenly I saw the largest dog raise its tail to the sky, and at that signal, all the rest stood up to follow the leader. I yelled for the crew, which was astounded by my hasty demand, and could not understand why I insisted that they film the shot." In a later scene in which the policeman makes love to the abandoned woman in the sweet shop, "the two assistant directors could not understand and were so outraged that they quit." All the same, actors and crew, working in intolerable heat, did collaborate. One memorable day Teshigahara enlisted them all, and joined them himself, to push and pull his old station wagon with the camera mounted within after it had become apparent to all that the motor of the car would produce too many vibrations for the camera. They labored mightily, pushing the car around a path bordering a pond that they themselves had cleared. Both Kanze and Teshigahara remember the incident—which Kanze calls "the epic of the five slaves"—as one of the high moments during the shooting, which took around fifty days. And they remember the heat. "On the black coal slag heaps the reflections produced fierce heat and pushed the temperature to over 50 degrees Celsius. Under the difficult conditions, everybody worked equally hard, without distinction or hierarchy."[4]

In *Pitfall*, Teshigahara demonstrated his strength as a visual artist, particularly in his sensitive treatment of light and environment. Almost immediately after the initial scene with the boy, Teshigahara films the vast white light behind the naturally desolate, dark landscape of the abandoned mine area. The white light becomes ominous with the appearance of the villain, a mysterious killer always impeccably clad in a white suit and gloves, whose figure stands sharp and threatening against the black slag heaps. The uncanny events in the film that culminate in the

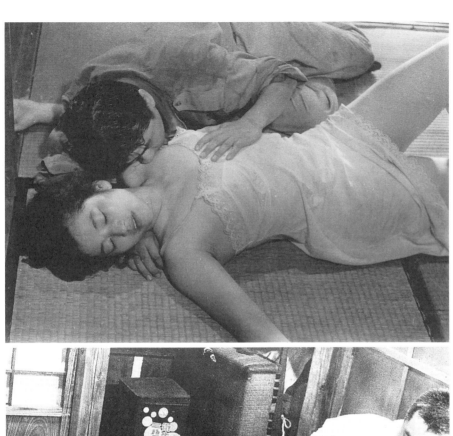

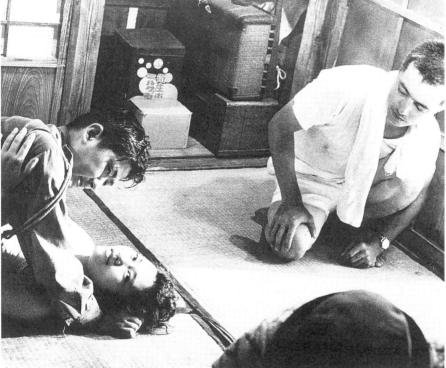

TOP: *Scene from* Pitfall; *policeman (played by Hideo Kanze) making love to a woman (played by Sumie Sasaki) in the sweet shop.* BOTTOM: *Hiroshi (at right) directing.*

Scene from Pitfall; *villain wearing a white suit and gloves.*

appearance of a ghost, or double, of a murdered character transpire in a climate of uneasiness reminiscent of Buñuel's work. Teshigahara even shows ants—Buñuel's hallmark—in the remains of the cookies in the sweet shop and a group of dusty masks recalling Ensor. Buñuel's mordant cruelty is also recalled in a scene in which Teshigahara films a child methodically tearing apart a tadpole.

Teshigahara's seemingly documentary technique, recording the abandoned mining town, is contradicted by the orchestrated appearance of ghosts that function much as a Greek chorus or the chorus in Noh drama. The tension between the camera-eye realism and the fantasy heightens the troubling situation. In real terms the film describes a nasty labor dispute. In allegorical terms it is an exposure of human frailty and psychological desolation. When it was shown soon after its completion by the Japan Art Theater Guild, the eminent film critic and historian Georges Sadoul saw it and invited Teshigahara to enter it in the 1962 Cannes film week of new directors. This was Teshigahara's first international recognition and encouraged him in his new métier.

Almost immediately after *Pitfall*, Abe published one of his finest novels, *The Woman in the Dunes*. Teshigahara quickly saw the visual possibilities in Abe's account of a high school teacher and amateur entomologist who gets lost in a vast landscape of dunes. Villagers find him and, as he has missed the last bus, lodge him with a widow who lives in a deep sand pit that she must dig out night and day. The school teacher, amused at first, soon realizes that he is a prisoner. Sullenly watching his hostess digging, he sees her as "quite like a beetle." Eventually, he begins his Sisyphus-like odyssey, joining her in her brutalizing task, reflecting on his situation, and finally, finding a means to make his life tolerable through the invention of a water trap. Although the novel is full of ambiguities and digressive speculations, and is by no means a clear parable of existence, it nonetheless drives relentlessly through the wilderness of sand, slowly making certain philosophic preoccupations of its author perceptible. Abe suggests that man's destiny is to make things. He must invent the means of subsisting. Since Teshigahara shared Abe's view, it was not difficult for him to find visual inspiration and to invent a visual counterpart to Abe's written word.

In the novel, the anti-hero—one of Abe's characteristic protagonists, who are almost always men in their mid-thirties, modestly employed, planted in meaningless lives that they rarely question—slowly reaches a heightened condition of self-awareness, but only when he has undertaken meaningful work, when finally he creates something. His slow enlightenment arrives as he begins to question the details in his life. The entrapped teacher, for instance, muses about newspapers, which in his isolation seem to him always "the same as usual," and he wonders if

> there had been a gap of a week, for there is almost nothing new to be found. If this was a window on the world outside, the glass was frosted . . . A tower of illusion, all of it, made of illusory brick and full of holes . . . But everyday life was exactly like the headlines. And so everybody, knowing the meaninglessness of existence, sets the center of his compass at his own home.[5]

Midway through the novel, as he thinks about recording his bizarre experience, the teacher conducts an imaginary dialogue with himself. "It's meaningless to trace only the surface of an event," he says; and his other self answers, "If you write, you're a writer, aren't you?" The teacher answers himself scornfully, "Is that what they call creative education . . . In spite of the fact that they haven't even made a pencil box by themselves?" Toward the midpoint of the novel, the author observes: "Work seemed something fundamental for man, something which enabled him to endure the aimless flight of time." Ruefully the teacher debates his situation, probing his motives, challenging himself with vital questions, trying to avoid the situation of *mauvaise foi*, accusing himself again and again, as when he says, "You want to distinguish between yourself and the puppets by making yourself a puppeteer." The climax of the novel is the invention of an ingenious device to trap water. The act of invention releases him. Having created something, he feels as if he had climbed to the top of a high tower. "He was still in a hole, but it seemed as if he were already outside."

Throughout the novel there are speculations about the nature of time, beginning in the first chapter with a lyrical introduction of the prevailing metaphor:

> As long as the winds blew, the rivers flowed, and the seas stirred, sand would be borne grain by grain from the earth, and like a living being, it would creep everywhere. . . . This image of the flowing sand made an indescribably exciting impact on the man. . . . Certainly sand was not suitable for life. Yet, was a stationary condition absolutely indispensable for existence?

Perhaps remembering romantic French literature of the nineteenth century with which all the Surrealists he had admired in his early youth were engaged, Abe's intermittent meditation on sand makes the assumption that "the only certain factor was its movement; sand was the antithesis of all form." It is Rimbaud's challenge in his letters of a seer, in which he exhorts future poets to go to the depths of experience and bring back material that, if it has form, give it form, and if it has no form, give it no form. Abe's challenge to himself in the novel is to bear the uncertainties, the anxieties produced by the shifting formlessness of matter. There are Goyaesque reveries in the novel, and Kafkaesque parables, as in the story of the guard who protected an imaginary castle:

> It could be anything: a factory, a bank, a gambling house . . . One day the long-expected enemy finally came. . . . The single guard, like a withered tree in the wilderness, had stood guarding an illusion.

Throughout the novel there are reminders of the ancient Greek maxim that the unexamined life is not worth living. Early in the novel the astonished prisoner asks: "Was it permissible to snare, exactly like a mouse or an insect, a man who had his certificate of medical insurance, someone who had paid his taxes, who was employed, and whose family records were in order?" The initial complacency of Abe's unhappy characters in all his novels is always the source of the plot, which unseats the creature of habit, and forces him on a difficult journey toward his essential humanity, his mysterious uniqueness, as envisioned by the Existentialists.

In his youth Abe had been an assiduous reader, especially of Heidegger and Karl Jaspers. Jaspers' voice lingers in Abe's speculations, as when the philosopher wrote, "Out of every position one may have adopted, i.e., out of every finitude, we are expelled; we are set whirling."[6] Or, "Man is fundamentally more than he can know about himself."[7] Jaspers declares the sources of philosophy to be wonder, doubt, and a sense of forsakeness. He emphasizes the importance of communication but insists that it must be "authentic" communication. In most of Abe's novels, the characters are in forlorn situations, but they, too, seek authentic means of communicating their often pitiful efforts at introspection.

Still, for all Abe's metaphysical overtones in his tale, he has not relinquished his responsibility as a realist—that is, someone who must see the world with eyes unencumbered by habit. The woman's curious acceptance of her fate as she labors ceaselessly to fend off the enemy of her homestead puts her at the center of the teacher's meditations, some of which circle around the issue most vital in Existentialist philosophy: the individual versus society. When the teacher asks what keeps the villagers moored in such a desperate environment, the woman points out that they couldn't find work elsewhere anyway.

One of the principal significant objects in the novel is the entomologist's lens. It offers the teacher the means to analyze the repetitions in life, and to ponder the paradoxical and pervasive feeling of linearity in man—the "one-way ticket" that fascinated Abe. Still, he says, "you can't really judge a mosaic unless you look at it from a distance."

Even though Abe wrote the screenplay, the creation of the film posed a great challenge to Teshigahara. He wrote, for instance, that "lines written by Kōbō Abe are not always on the same surface as the situation.

Vernacular words and abstract speech appear together to manifest the theme in an inductive way."[8] His task was to capture the mood and find visual analogues for the atmosphere of tension between the two major characters. Since Abe's underlying themes were important to Teshigahara, whose point of view had developed along similar lines during the decade of their friendship, his problem was to endow the allegorical aspects of the novel with sufficient visual illumination, while not losing the dramatic character of the film. He was eminently successful as he carefully imagined vantage points, objects, and the flow of interaction between actress and actor.

One of his most inspired decisions was to enlist a gifted and intelligent actress, Kyōko Kishida as the lead. With her small upright figure, her huge expressive eyes, and uncommonly plastic face, Kishida provided a foil to the initially stiff visitor, played by Eiiji Okada. Teshigahara, instinctively drawn to the Existentialist vision of human loneliness and the longing for solidarity, needed Kishida's enigmatic face and her brilliantly conceived physical gestures. The actress grasped the situation and built the complexities of character that were hidden behind the appearance of a simple, unlettered village woman.

Teshigahara, who always seeks the illuminating moment while shooting, and respects high moments of improvisation, could depend on Kishida's intelligence and dramatic invention. Not everyone working with him could, as his experience in shooting *Pitfall* proved. Kishida recalls the vicissitudes of the difficult scene-by-scene construction of the film with admiration for Teshigahara's "flexibility." She describes the long scene of the meal the woman prepares, encumbered by intermittent spills of sand. There was, as usual, no rehearsal. At one point, Okada sneezed and the rice went flying. "I immediately improvised by picking up the grains of rice one by one, but to Teshigahara's chagrin, the cameraman didn't shoot it, and Teshigahara was very angry."

Teshigahara admired Abe's "approach to reality" which he says always begins with a concrete detail. He develops character through details. As an admirer of Buñuel, and the French and Italian neo-realists, and above all, as a skilled painter, Teshigahara's use of detail was extraordinary. The tension in the flow of *The Woman in the Dunes* is achieved through his careful measuring out of telling details against the sea of amorphous sand grains. His immersion in the metaphor of sand was total. When he wrote about his experience filming *The Woman in the Dunes*, he described how tiny grains of sand sneaked in everywhere as if alive, and pricked my eyes like sharp stones. The sand turned into a sharp knife in a strong wind. I meant to breathe clear air but the grittiness of the sand covered my tongue. The sand looked like grains under a magnifying glass, but it felt as though it had sharp pointed edges. In the course of struggling with the sand, I realized that sand flows like liquid, possesses will, and represents beauty and solitude. My creativity was stirred by the struggle with the sharply pointed, stinging sand.[9]

From the beginning, the film is visually striking. It opens with titles in large, very strong calligraphy, and continues with a montage of documents with official stamps, fingerprints, and a catalogue of bureaucratically controlled aspects of life. For the titles, Teshigahara enlisted his old friend, Kiyoshi Awazu, who had already worked with him on *Pitfall* and had done striking posters for *José Torres*. Awazu, two years younger than Teshigahara, is one of a dozen members of his generation to whom Teshigahara returns regularly in his collaborations, and who share his feelings about the nature of art, and sometimes play bit parts in his films. Awazu has written of his generation:

Artists of my generation tend to try things that are beyond their genres. A crossbreeding of different styles results and distinctions among various art forms become blurred. Artists often feel that they can leap into different genres and explore an unknown world. If we take fine art and graphic design more openly, a theatrical space is also an artistic space. But in today's age of specialization, it might be only us, the "après-guerre" generation who started from a wide stretch of burned ruins, that have this conception about artistic styles.[10]

Teshigahara introduces his motif with close-ups of sand and sounds of sand. The teacher is seen from behind, scrambling in the dune which rises into infinity with no horizon—one of the few and therefore crucial long shots in the film. Then Teshigahara begins his inspired catalogue of the effects of sand, portrayed at times as if it were smoke, and at other times as if it were the sea. Close-ups of wood grain, or the structure and texture of a caterpillar, are juxtaposed with close-ups of the granular film that sheathes Kishida's body, or Okada's glasses and personal effects. Gradually, as the relationship between the oddly matched couple deepens, Teshigahara's camera surveys their realm with increasing attention—the dilapidated cottage, utensils, tatami mats and headcloths, as well as the small area outside in the shadow of the sand pit. For the film's climax, Teshigahara invented a scene that was not in the script, a kind of Witches' Sabbath, in which the villagers, in grotesque wooden masks, watch the couple making love, while *Gojinju* drums in frighteningly intense pitches hasten them toward climax.

The film can be called a masterpiece, since it has endured many years, and those who have seen it more than once always report on its immediacy and presence so many years after it was created. Teshigahara's gifts as a visual artist are eminently displayed here. When I first saw the film I wrote:

> Teshigahara's *Woman in the Dunes* is saturated with techniques common to the visual plastic arts. His close-ups of sand, grain by grain, recalls Miró's blade-by-blade close-ups of grass. His way of focusing on an insect, so that it takes up the whole screen and transforms itself into an attenuated, hardly identifiable object, is similar to many approaches in metamorphic or organic abstraction—that of Arshile Gorky for instance.[11]

More recently, a film critic in *Le Monde* responded to the film, calling it "total splendor" that draws upon a universe of infinite richness. The critic points out that at the time it was first shown, critics invoked, justly, Kafka, Beckett and Camus. They could also have cited *Robinson Crusoe* and *Woyzcek*:

> The art of the director consists in explaining nothing; letting the inexorable machine of the capture, rebellion, desire, fatigue, submission and compromise function to the point of madness. In the leitmotif of abstract images of rills of sand, all the metaphors are there: those of passing time, of the esprit that loses itself, of the infinite and the immense, of telluric powers and children's games. Teshigahara never lingers or underlines, he is always already in a new register, intimist, social, mythological, erotic, fantastic, moral, or psychological . . . Rarely has a film thus invented its own texture, its own gestures and its own graphism . . . [12]

Two scenes from Woman in the Dunes *(1964); a high school teacher and amateur entomologist (played by Eiji Okada) sets off in search of insects in the sand dunes.*

Widow (Kyōko Kishida) and school teacher (Eiji Okada) outside her dilapidated hut amid the dunes.

Teshigahara would turn out two more films based on Abe's novels, with the film adaptations written by Abe himself, but they were not received with comparable enthusiasm. It is not difficult to see why: both the novels are far more abstract and diffuse, and there is no single metaphor to which Teshigahara could address his specific visual abilities. It was far more difficult to make a screenplay of *The Face of Another*, whose first sentence is:

> At last you have come, threading your way through the endless passages of the maze. With a map you got from *him* you have finally found your way to my hideaway—the first room at the top of the creaking, harmonium-pedal stairs.[13]

The story is about a middle-level employee of a chemical factory whose face has been burned beyond recognition, and who dons a mask created by a plastic surgeon. With the face of another, he tries to seduce his wife, who succumbs, to his great chagrin, and when he reproaches her, she leaves him, suggesting that she has known all along it was he. In his fury the man goes back to the psychiatrist who first induced him to wear the mask and attacks him with a knife.

Teshigahara tried to sustain the symbolic level of the story by asking his friend Isozaki to design the interiors. Isozaki joined Teshigahara in his search for the outdoor sites and made sketches for the surrealistic interior of the doctor's office (in which Kishida would move, creating an enigmatic character, perhaps wise nurse, perhaps evil accomplice). The eventual set, although thoroughly surrealistic as Teshigahara intended, was not well connected in the editing with other scenes. The obviousness of the symbolism of the mask could not be dispelled, even though there are many shots throughout the film of street scenes, cafes, and apartments that bear the improvisatory singularity of Teshigahara's eye.

The final Abe novel Teshigahara shot was a metaphysical detective story filmed with the title *The Man Without a Map* and based on the novel published in English as *The Ruined Map*. In the book, which has an epigraph, "The City—a bounded infinity. A labyrinth where you are never lost," Abe traces the disappearance of one of his typical characters, a man in his thirties who is "section head for sales and expansion;" in other words, a typical postwar company man. Abe's social concerns soon emerge. The housing project in which the vanished salesman lived

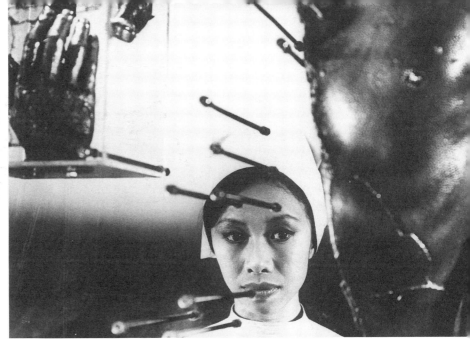

Three scenes from The Face of Another *(1966); nurse (Kyōko Kishida) in the doctor's office.*

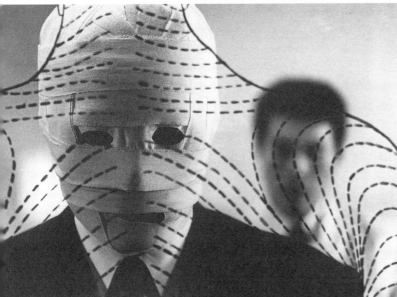

Man wearing a face mask.

The street scene.

Kōbō Abe (left) with Etsuko Ichihara and Shintarō Katsu, who played the roles of the woman whose husband disappeared and the private investigator in The Man Without a Map.

Scene from The Man Without a Map; *laborers fighting.*

is described as "this human filing cabinet with its endless filing-card apartments."[14] He has the detective protagonist walk thirty-two paces from the corner of Building Three, retracing the missing man's steps as he "baldly and irreversibly stepped across a chasm, turning his back on the world." The wife, who had hired the detective, quotes her perhaps nonexistent brother saying, "He says a single map for life is all you need. The world is a forest, a woods, full of wild beasts and poisonous insects. You should only go through places where everyone goes, places that are considered absolutely safe." Abe's attention turns to the distant suburbs where endless new, anonymous-looking apartments spring up, and where small speculators at first prosper and then are ruined as huge corporations crush them, caught as they are "in the coils of events."

Toward the end of the novel, after a wild encounter with gangs of criminals, the detective, who has lost his job but keeps searching for the identity of his quarry, is again in the dark street; "most of the commuters were already in place in the filing drawer houses" and he is struck, as often in Abe's tales, with amnesia. "I began walking, relying on a map I did not comprehend." The last chapter is almost identical with the 1966 story "Beyond the Curve," but in the story, the cafe girl says, "You can't try to understand everything, you know," to which the author says: "Maybe so. Maybe it was enough to understand this much. Maybe the sense of continuity I had had in front of that curve—the sense that everything up to then was normal—had itself been a strange dream."[15]

The old motif of the dream within a dream was not sufficient to hold the screenplay together, and although Teshigahara's frequent moving shots of the city, his deft use of mirrors—car mirrors, side mirrors, reflections of the detective's face on a shiny plastic table—and his views of Tokyo streets with the stampede of feet and clutter of traffic were frequently of exceptional quality, the film never achieved the seamless texture of *Woman in the Dunes*. There were splendid high moments, such as the fiery conflagration, gang fight, and rape in a night scene, and the Buñuel-like shot of a dead dog, but the philosophic or allegorical overtones of Abe's original remained elusive.

NOTES

1 Makoto Ōoka, *The Colors of Poetry: Essays on Classic Japanese Verse*, trans. Takako and Thomas V. Lento, Oakland Univ., Michigan, 1991, p. 28.

2 Mellen, *Voices from the Japanese Cinema*, p. 145.

3 Natsume Sōseki, *Kokoro*, trans. Edwin McClellan, Tokyo, 1969, p. 30.

4 Teshigahara, *Furuta Oribe*.

5 Kōbō Abe, *The Woman in the Dunes*, trans. E. Dale Saunders, New York, 1991, p. 93.

6 Karl Jaspers, *Way to Wisdom*, London, 1951, p. 63.

7 Ibid., p. 63.

8 Teshigahara, *Furuta Oribe*.

9 Teshigahara, *Furuta Oribe*.

10 *The Works of Kiyoshi Awazu*, Tokyo, 1989, p. 149.

11 Dore Ashton, *A Reading of Modern Art*, Cleveland, 1971, p. 197.

12 J.M.F., *Le Monde*, July 23, 1993.

13 Kōbō Abe, *The Face of Another*, New York, 1966.

14 Kōbō Abe, *The Ruined Map*, New York, 1969, p. 8.

15 Kōbō Abe, *Beyond the Curve*, trans. Juliet Winters Carpenter, Tokyo, 1991, p. 247.

6

*A*ll during the filming of the Kōbō Abe scripts, Teshigahara had
been busy coordinating the plethora of vanguard events at
Sōgetsu Hall, in the course of which he was in close rapport
with his friend, the composer Tōru Takemitsu. Many of the most important events had been in music and performance art, in which Takemitsu
played an important role as mentor. It was natural for Teshigahara to
turn to him for the music that was a notable element in all the films
from *José Torres* onward. For *Pitfall*, for instance, Takemitsu asked Toshi
Ichiyanagi and Yuji Takahashi to improvise on the prepared piano and
harpsichord, probably the first time ever John Cage's methods were
adapted to film. Ichiyanagi, who had been one of the earliest postwar
artists to seek his education in New York, studied classical music at
Julliard, where Robert Mann, founder of the Julliard String Quartet,
remembers him as a highly gifted student who used to take him to
Japanese restaurants with a "mousy and shy girl" who soon became
famous as Yōko Ono. It was through Ichiyanagi that Cage and Merce
Cunningham were invited to Sōgetsu, and Takemitsu participated
in several performance events—or happenings—on Sōgetsu's stage: he
appeared with Akiyama and Ichiyanagi in May 1964 in *Time Perspective*
and with Cage himself, in November 1964, in *Blue Aurora*.

Takemitsu's role as composer, and often as director of sound, in
Teshigahara's films was unique. Teshigahara had, and still has, an
absolute confidence in Takemitsu who, he says, always took an intense
interest in the film from the outset, visiting location sites and watching

Tōru Takemitsu.

the filming. He often studied the takes from each day's work and immersed himself in every aspect of the ensemble's work. Without fail, Takemitsu supplied the kind of counterpart that Teshigahara needed, the "collision" of sound and image that Teshigahara sought. Through close collaboration, which seems typical of this generation, many unexpected ideas were spawned amongst a handful of gifted artists in every domain. The poet Ōoka, friend and collaborator of both Takemitsu and Teshigahara, in his tribute to Takemitsu, who had set one of his poems, "Coral Island," to music, wrote that he felt the energy of words transformed into the energy of sound; he realized through Takemitsu that "words are crystals made of sounds."[1] Takemitsu writing about Teshigahara as film director reported that he was constantly reminded of his own powerlessness. "The images themselves reverberate with a distinct and fertile sound, and the music can play only an adjunct role, bringing into sharper focus the sounds that the images emit."[2]

Takemitsu's friendship with Teshigahara entailed more than a working relationship on specific films. They shared in the agitated struggle to find a balance between their avowed hatred for the kind of hierarchies that had blighted their childhood and an attraction to the best in their own Japanese tradition. Both men began with a determined resistance to the old ways and later evolved toward a heterogeneous view, absorbing much from the West, and particularly from the United States, but adapting it to what they could retrieve from the East. In music, according to the music critic, Akiyama, one of the most important figures was John Cage, a messenger from New York bringing his own attitude toward Zen Buddhism back to Japan, making it palatable to the young who had rejected it initially. "He taught them that they could look at old things and new things as equal."[3]

Like most of the others in Teshigahara's circle, Takemitsu had been attentive to Takiguchi, whose authority as a Surrealist was unquestioned. Takiguchi had functioned as a critic, poet, and later, visual artist, since the 1930s. During the first years after the war, he was committed to encouraging the new generation in its experimental efforts, and many a young artist was inspired by his personality. Takemitsu valued Takiguchi's absolute integrity. Takiguchi received younger artists, as one critic said, the way Mallarmé did, in an informal weekly salon. Takemitsu, who was a principal founder of the Jikken Kōbō group in 1951, carried into the group activity many of Takiguchi's dynamic ideas on the function of the arts. Above all, Takiguchi was a source of a rich array of references to Europe, particularly the Europe of iconoclasts such as Paul Eluard and André Breton, but also, Rainer Maria Rilke. (Takemitsu would later say he had been influenced by Rilke's "Weltinnerraum.")

Most of the young experimental artists in the circle around both Takiguchi and Okamoto—veterans of the Surrealist era—had been nurtured on the avant-garde literature of the nineteenth century as revived by the French Surrealists in the twentieth century. Arata Isozaki, for instance, when he came to Tokyo in 1950 was armed, he says, with the knowledge of only two books: the poems of Arthur Rimbaud and *Modern Art* by Takiguchi. Rimbaud had been translated by Hideo Kobayashi (1902–1983), whose critical writings often centered on Rimbaud, Baudelaire, and Paul Valéry, and in later years, Dostoyevsky. Important ideas, that would deeply affect the foundation of the first postwar avant-garde, were often culled from conversations with Takiguchi. Judging by statements of artists in various areas of the arts, it would seem that the Surrealist examination of synaesthesia in both their poetry and critical writings was of particular importance. Takemitsu could find in Takiguchi's discourse complements to his own discoveries, such as the music of Debussy, who "seeks many points of focus and many gradations of color" and always "combines several things at the same time."[4]

Takemitsu's restless inquiry into the sources of modern art in all

Shūzō Takiguchi.

media was thorough. He is a person who, as André Breton recommended, is always *disponible*, available to new experiences and eager to follow the trails of almost anything—musical composition, poem, painting, calligraphy, garden—that has attracted his attention. In the discussions of the Jikken Kōbō group, the inquiries ranged from close study of the early pioneers of Western modern music such as Arnold Schoenberg, Alban Berg, and Anton von Webern, to the peculiarities of Noh and *gagaku*, with comparison of spatiality and tonal color.

The influence of Takiguchi, and tangentially Okamoto, kept the young composers alert to the other arts, seeking ways to fuse them, while Takiguchi always encouraged them in their ever-widening quest for the unorthodox. Takiguchi's importance in Takemitsu's development is signalled by a composition worked on between 1952 and 1959, based on a poem by Takiguchi titled *Uninterrupted Rests*. The contributions of the elder experimentalists can perhaps be seen in an essay Takemitsu wrote many years later in which he extols contradictions: "I would prefer, in fact, to deepen many of the contradictions and make them more vivid."[5] Like Teshigahara, Takemitsu has been faithful to the precepts stressed by Okamoto; above all, the necessity of enduring conflicting thoughts.

Early in the 1950s, the Takemitsu group was engaged in seeking ways to work with audio-visual performance, which would bear fruit only in the 1960s, when they were tempted by electronic music. Takemitsu himself, as early as 1956, asked the poet Shuntarō Tanikawa to give him a text for setting to music. Tanikawa gave him a one word text: *ai*, which in Japanese means "love." Takemitsu's composition, *Vocalism A.I.*, 1956, stressed the two-syllable word in many registers with each phoneme pronounced by two actors in his composition for magnetic tape, while, as already noted, *Water Music* of 1960 is a montage of natural water sounds.

Takemitsu was always interested in the "reciprocal action" between orient and occident (such as the impact of eastern modes on Debussy and Ravel) and its re-importation to Japan. A man of nervous intensity, full of curiosity, Takemitsu understood how important it was to risk being labeled an eclectic in the interest of attaining to the universal— an aspiration shared, to this day, with Teshigahara. Both artists are constantly exploring, questioning, noting the curious ways the arts converge in different cultures. In this they were not alone. Others were seeking parallel paths, as revealed in an anecdote about Edgard Varèse, a composer who particularly interested young Japanese artists.

In the important Karuizawa festival in 1958, Varèse's music had been played along with works of Bartók, Schoenberg, and Webern. That same year a young Japanese composer, Michiko Toyama, who was studying in New York, was advised by John Cage to seek out Varèse. To the author Fernand Ouellette, who was writing the first full-length study of Varèse, she wrote in 1960 that when she saw scores for Varèse's *Integrale* and *Octandre*, she was immediately struck with the likeness to *gagaku*. Shortly after her first visit, they were both at a party where some *gagaku* musicians were to perform. "At my invitation, the Master came over and took a look at my score: 'Your music is very much like *gagaku*'."[6] Varèse was overjoyed and remarked, "It happened without my knowing anything about *gagaku*." Shortly after, Toyama visited again and found him at work studying the frequency range of the *shō*, the instrument of seventeen bamboo pipes, like a mouth organ, that can produce simultaneous multiple sounds.

The Jikken Kōbō group was actively engaged during the late 1950s in the perplexing activity of sorting out many artistic voices, while many of their young contemporaries were swept up in the great controversy centering on the renewal of the security treaty with the United States. The streets of Tokyo saw several mass demonstrations in 1960 that could not fail to affect the spirits of young artists.

It was around then that Takemitsu began reconsidering his point of view concerning culture and identity. He had given several explanations of the origin of his turn to his own tradition. In one he described attending a *bunraku* performance and being moved when he heard the sound of the wide-necked *shamisen*. While still working in various idioms, including aleatoric and atonal languages adapted from Western sources, Takemitsu was moving toward a different "stream of sounds"— the sounds and silences of non-urban spaces. It was probably around 1961 that he turned his attention to the Japanese garden, and like his much older friend Isamu Noguchi, went back to the original source, the fourteenth-century monk, Musō Soseki. Both Takemitsu and Teshigahara had, by then, established a warm friendship with Noguchi, whose admonitions to look to their own tradition gradually began to seem essential.

In the traditional Japanese garden, where each stone, rock, and tree is carefully considered in terms of an imagined space that forms a continuum, sounds are also governed by the total design. The wonderful clack of the bamboo water collector, which falls when it is sufficiently full, and the murmur of brooks or the smooth silence of ponds, are all consciously considered in the garden-artist's imagination.

Takemitsu was moved around 1962 to write a number of essays under the title *Nature and Music*, defying the vanguard tendency to reject the cliché about the Japanese being closer to nature. It was then that he began his long meditation on the fundamental difference between Japanese and Western perceptions of sound and studied the *biwa* in terms of a poetic conception of "touch," or *sawari*. Thirty years later he would still be musing on these problems, which as he underlined in his lecture at Columbia University, would finally locate themselves in the broader notion of "the human condition."[7] In 1963–1966, he composed *Arc*, for which he enunciated his notion of a garden first in a drawing— a drawing almost certainly inspired by his discovery of Musō, and perhaps encouraged by his acquaintance with the work of John Cage.

Cage's presence in the mind of Takemitsu and many others was, in a way, the conducting wire leading back to Japan, since Cage himself was a great enthusiast of the Zen scholar Daisetz Suzuki and put a high value on nature and natural sounds. At the same time, Cage ignored the boundaries of the arts and never hesitated to turn to the word when he felt the need. His poetic utterances bestirred his young colleagues, and Takemitsu, already in close association with poets, among them Ōoka, turned his attention to the word. His essays in the mid-1960s refer often to *kotoba*—the word—and investigate the sonorous qualities of individual words in various unsophisticated, sometimes preliterate societies. His concerns during the years when he and Teshigahara were working together on films and planning events for Sōgetsu Hall were also Teshigahara's concerns.

Takemitsu, with his taste for poetry (he shared with Noguchi a great regard for William Blake) read widely, from James Joyce to Gaston Bachelard—that great reader whose thoughts so often inhabited spaces that could only be imagined. Takemitsu developed ever more specifically his notion that there is reciprocity in cultures and among individuals. And he, and several of the others, began to explore the Japanese concept of *ma* as living space, "the mother of sound," as Takemitsu interpreted it.

Many years later (1978), Isozaki would produce an extraordinary exhibition illustrating the notion of *ma* which summed up the kinds of inquiries Takemitsu, Teshigahara, and Ōoka, to name a few, had begun during the 1960s and continued after. Isozaki concluded that *ma* was indeed a special approach to the definition of space developed by the Japanese. It was, as Isozaki maintained, an idea of space/time endemic to Japanese art since its origins, that the West had only recently begun to consider. Whether or not *ma* is particularly Japanese, the young artists who began to think about it could be sure that it was an authentic source from their own culture and were greatly inspired by it. Ōoka, in a poem, reflected the preoccupation of his generation with *ma*. The epigraph of the poem is:

> A Questionnaire: Among how many richly useful Japanese words is the word "*ma*" which signifies "interval" in time and space. What does "*ma*" mean in your work?

Ōoka's answer in a number of stanzas begins:

> Come to think of it,
> in writing poems
> I've never even considered
> "*ma*".

He suggests that for the time spent trying to pin down "*ma*," the word will slip out of your grasp, adding:

If you think of "*ma*"
    as something between one thing and another,
    you're wrong.

He concludes:

When breathing weaves colors into "*ma*"
    all of "*ma*"
    emerges from within me.
Because it is shapeless,
    it becomes the source of all shapes,
    which is a *force*.[8]

At the same time, Takemitsu, probably through Noguchi, became interested in the American designer and philosopher R. Buckminster Fuller, whose constant allusions to the "cosmic egg" and whose conviction that there could be something he referred to as "universal culture" pulled against the tendency to debate the specific and specifically non-universal in the arts of Japan.

Takemitsu took on the task of reiterating the need to hold both in uneasy balance. These attitudes persist in all the arts in Japan, creating an almost chronic condition of uncertainty on the one side, and contentious dogmatism on the other. For musicians, who traveled and performed elsewhere, the cultural issues first broached in the 1960s remained constant, as Ichiyanagi demonstrated when he answered a reporter from the *The New York Times* asking about what he was seeking in his music in 1990: "a certain awareness that comes from looking at Japanese tradition from a contemporary viewpoint as well as a search for the logic and sensitivity of the East that has existed in the past and is now lost."[9]

The sense of loss, so often mentioned among artists of Teshigahara's generation, grew rather than diminished as events—historical, political, social, and finally, aesthetic—caught up with them. Both Teshigahara and Takemitsu, hard at work making Kōbō Abe's vision filmically audible and visible, from 1962 to 1968, were in an exhausting quest for affirmation of their intuitive choices and often went to the same sources. Both would eventually take their native traditions into their world views, and both remained faithful to certain tenets of the Existentialist movement: most particularly, the insistence that the individual exists vis-à-vis the "other"; that the "human condition" requires the making of something; the acknowledgment of reciprocity as a force in nature; and the fight against death (which Takemitsu often equates with silence).

Teshigahara's constancy in his beliefs, despite the many turnings his work has taken, can be gauged in his statements over a long period. In the early 1970s, he told Mellen that what he was filming in *The Face of Another* was "the magnitude of human isolation and loneliness."[10] More than a decade later, he is quoted by Peter Grilli, saying "history and cultural problems may change over time but fundamental human problems do not."[11]

NOTES

1   Makoto Ōoka, "A Few Observations Concerning Toru Takemitsu," in Kuniharu Akiyama, *Tōru Takemitsu*, Tokyo, 1981.

2   Akiyama, *Tōru Takemitsu*.

3   Akiyama, *Tōru Takemitsu*.

4   Ōtake, *Creative Sources*, p. 7.

5   Tōru Takemitsu, "A Mirror and an Egg," trans. Shōko Aki and Daniel Starr, Sōgetsu Archives, p. 3.

6   Michiko Toyama, letter to Fernand Ouellette, Aug. 31, 1960, quoted in Ouellette, *Edgard Varèse*, trans. Derek Coltman, New York, 1968.

7   Tōru Takemitsu, lecture at Columbia University, "Higashi no Oto," New York, Nov. 14, 1989.

8   Makoto Ōoka, *Elegy and Benediction. Selected Poems 1947–1989*, trans. William I. Elliott, and Kazuo Kawamura, Honolulu, 1991, p. 73.

9   Raphael Mostel, "Japanese Composers Delve into the Past for their Futures," *The New York Times*, Feb. 18, 1990, p. H25.

10   Mellen, *Voices from the Japanese Cinema*, p. 174.

11   Peter Grilli, "After 17 Years, a Director Reappears," *The New York Times*, Sept. 24, 1989, p. H15.

7

During the 1960s, what Teshigahara called "fundamental human problems" were often overshadowed by tumultuous events. The drumbeat of rebellion became paroxysmic as the decade drew to a close. There was an increasingly hectic, anarchic coloration to the artistic events in Sōgetsu Hall that seemed to reflect the growing tension between aesthetics and political action. Under the stress of particularly difficult political developments, artists seemed to feel much the way Kōbō Abe had felt in the first years after the war, as he wrote in an autobiographical memoir:

> Then, suddenly the war was over, and a vicious anarchy reigned. The state of anarchy made me anxious and afraid, but at the same time I suspect it thrilled me too, aroused my hopes. At least that terrific wall of authority had disappeared.[1]

Although Teshigahara had averted his gaze from the furious ideological arguments of many of his peers after his voyage to Europe and America, remaining aloof became increasingly difficult. Many of his friends were embroiled in political protests. Artists experienced more urgently an unwillingness to tread purely aesthetic paths in the traditional way. A very old dilemma became salient once again, and some, at least, reacted as did the Kamakura warrior around 1300 in *Tale of Obusuma Saburō* which tells of two brothers in a time of political upheaval. One is an aesthete who composes poetry and plays the flute; the other is a practical warrior who declares:

What is the use of filling one's heart with thoughts of the moon or flowers, or composing verse, or plucking a lute? The ability to strum a zither or blow a flute doesn't count for much on the battlefield.[2]

The events that challenged and unsettled artists began with mass demonstrations in 1960 against the renewed security treaty with the United States which many Japanese citizens feared would strengthen the hand of the military. After the first explosion, there was a lull as Tokyo engaged in vast rebuilding and refurbishing for the 1964 Olympics, an activity that successfully distracted its citizens until the Tonkin Gulf incident of August 2, 1964, and the American reprisal attack on North Vietnam. On August 10th, a large rally bringing together the Communist and Socialist parties, as well as 135 other organizations, sounded the deep alarm over the possibility of Japanese complicity in a new war. By February 1965, the Americans were bombing North Vietnam, and by March, they were fully committed to the war which, as the peace advocates in Japan understood, required indirect support from Japan in the form of military bases and supplies.

On April 24, 1965, a group of artists, writers, scholars, and other professionals demonstrated in Shimizudani Park. Among the founding members of Beheiren, which organized this and subsequent protests, were Kenzaburō Ōe, Hiroshi Noma, Shūji Terayama, and Tarō Okamoto. The loosely organized group was initiated by them, together with a charismatic writer, Makoto Oda. Though relatively small as Tokyo demonstrations went, the event was to be the beginning of an ongoing peace movement. That day, participants handed out leaflets in which they asked spectators "to please take part as ordinary citizens" in a movement for peace in Vietnam, self-determination for the Vietnamese, and an end of Japan's complicity in the war. Oda, whom Thomas R. H. Havens describes as a man who "declined fixed dogmas in favor of freedom of personal choice, in a manner remarkably similar to the existential art of Jūrō Kara,"[3] would soon lead the rather amorphous movement, called Beheiren, in the direction of international solidarity. Although not many of the artists performing in Sōgetsu were active in Beheiren, they often shared principles.

The avant-garde generally saw protest in different terms, more in keeping with the old idea of *épater la bourgeoisie*, but they could scarcely ignore the mounting violence in the streets of Tokyo as the student movement became increasingly restive, and as the police more and more often provoked or responded violently to political melees. By 1968, when there were protests all over the world, Tokyo's artists showed solidarity both by participating in an exhibition, "Anti-War and Liberation," organized by Hariu, and by signing a petition—600 signatures—"opposed to American aggression in Vietnam." By 1969, a rally at Hibiya Park drew almost 70,000 protestors and vigorous actions by riot police.

In such an agitated moment, it was hard for artists to retreat. Teshigahara was no exception. He watched carefully when, after 1967, Beheiren began helping military personnel at American bases to protest and defect, and gradually formed the decision to devote his next film to the subject.

As an *obbligato* to the visible disruption in Tokyo's daily life, the efforts of artists who preferred to remain independent of mass movements also became more shrill. Those activities at Sōgetsu Hall and elsewhere in Tokyo which are generally collected under the rubric of "anti-art" took a distinctly provocative turn. The opening salvo came in the form of yet another artists' group (despite the emphasis on nonconformity, the Japanese art world was still functioning in the old way of groups and leaders), this one organized by Genpei Akasegawa (with whom Teshigahara would collaborate many years later on the film script for *Rikyū*) together with Shūsaku Arakawa and nine young artists who had showed in the most avant-garde annual, the Yomiuri Independent show.

In a memoir that begins, "I will never be able to forget 1960," Akasegawa writes that it was "the year the destructively energetic Neo-Dada art group was born; it was also the year of the first fatality in the anti-U.S. demonstrations."[4] Called the "Neo-Dada Organizers," the group held its first show in April 1960. Akasegawa quotes from a draft by Ushio Shinohara of the group's manifesto, sounding the note of violent disillusion these young artists were experiencing:

> In whatever way we fantasize about what our future may be in 1960—about the way that one atomic explosion will lightheartedly resolve everything—Picasso's fighting bulls move us now no more than the blood splattered from a run-over stray cat. We enter the ring on an Earth gone mad in this twentieth

century—the century which has stamped on serious works of art. The only way we will be spared the massacre is to turn the slaughterers on themselves.[5]

Akasegawa, in retrospect, connects the "events" the group staged frequently throughout the year with what he calls "a much wider social force" coming from "a nationwide mass struggle against the revision of the U.S.–Japan security treaty." Hariu briefly describes their activities:

> They performed in studios, galleries, and parks, lining up scrap and rubbish, reading statements, banging metal basins, playing jazz tapes, putting their heads in buckets and shouting, breaking beer bottles or chairs by karate . . . [6]

The group, as Akasegawa notes, soon broke up, but by 1963, he, Jirō Takamatsu, and Natsuyuki Nakanishi formed another which they called "Hi-Red Center." "Although we were painters, we had all deviated from painting as a fixed form. We were pointed towards this neither by art, music, theater, politics, or business as such, but apparently all of these. Every last issue of our lives was affected."[7]

Some of their activities took place in the streets of Tokyo where astonished onlookers were engaged, often unwillingly, in the events, one of which was a cleanup operation in the streets of Tokyo, and others, in which they threw things, including enormous pieces of cloth, from the tops of buildings. Later assessments of the importance of these activities, which were not entirely bereft of humor, point out that Okamoto was a sympathetic accomplice to the activities, which in many ways reflected his contention in early years that, "Utter nonsense may have more power to change social reality than seriousness."

Kaidō Kazu, for instance, believes that the Japanese Neo-Dadaists differed from their American counterparts because of their social and political concerns. "It is now clear that there was an underlying spirit of radicalism and anti-authoritarianism in postwar Japanese avant-garde art."[8] But Akasegawa himself wavers in his claims of serious political commitment and finally enunciates a point of view closer to nineteenth-century Nihilism than to the earnest intentions of older figures such as Okamoto and Hanada.

One of their more gnomic utterances was printed on the tickets for an event in which they declared themselves "for Art minus Art." The whole idea of anti-art came to be seen as a homeopathic antidote to the madness of the real world, and in its various manifestations in Japan, competed with real "happenings" such as the violent mass demonstrations.

There were many levels of dissidence during those years, ranging from often sophomoric declarations against anything that might be called "art" to serious attempts to open the arts to the vicissitudes of daily life. The true Dada heritage from the years around the end of the First World War was known only from books, but some of the major players of the period were still alive and enjoying a newfound notoriety. Marcel Duchamp, the éminence grise of the New York Dada tradition, was very much on the minds of the young Japanese musicians around John Cage, as he was in the thoughts of such new celebrities in New York as Jasper Johns and Robert Rauschenberg. His influence hovered over the more unorthodox group that in the early 1960s, under the guidance of George Maciunas, announced themselves as an international force called Fluxus. These groupings in New York, which tended to include all the arts, overflowing boundaries between theatrical performance and

Jasper Johns in Tokyo, 1964.

musical performance, poetry and music, painting and dancing, were aware of similar groupings in Europe and Japan, and soon established active ties. At the heart of nearly every "happening" or performance was the challenge to art itself, the testing of the limits, and the Ubu-like desire to destroy everything in order to reconstruct something pure.

When, for instance, John Cage wrote an article on Robert Rauschenberg for an international art magazine, he was clear about his message, describing Rauschenberg's "combines" as "a situation involving multiplicity."[9] Perhaps, after all, he wrote, there is no message. "In that case, one is saved the trouble of having to reply. As the lady said, 'Well, if it isn't art, then I like it.'" The young Japanese artists, musicians and dancers who had made their way to New York agreed, Ichiyanagi and Yōko Ono above all. They returned to Japan to bring their non-message of non-art to the art world in Tokyo, and naturally, found their theater at Teshigahara's Sōgetsu.

Although there were attempts to find precedents in the nonrational traditions of extremist Zen monks, most Japanese critics regarded the Neo-Dada storm as an international phenomenon peculiar to the twentieth century. They responded with various degrees of shock and irritation to Ichiyanagi's performances using Cage's unorthodox methods of wringing sounds from the innards of a piano, and even more to Yōko Ono's first performance at Sōgetsu on May 24, 1962. Akiyama quotes from the only entirely favorable review in the *Asahi Journal*, which likened her performance to that of John Cage and said that, "this is not a rare rebellion against art, but the extremely natural act of testing, on the same level as daily life, as in life equals not knowing the boundaries of art."[10]

Yōko Ono's event brought together many young artists, composers, designers, painters, and dancers, including Akasegawa, Akiyama, and Hijikata, who would soon dazzle his audiences with his Butoh troupe. Apart from Yōko Ono's performance at the piano, striking its keys repeatedly with her elbows, there was her "opera," in which all the performers read aloud newspapers from all over the world against a background of a tape of a speech by Adolph Hitler. "The entire opera was performed without the use of any musical instruments," the Asahi account says. "Men with their limbs bound together or tied down to chairs could be seen moving on the dimly lit stage. Hands and feet grew out from the linen backstage curtain, moving as if in search of something.

In front, a French man and Japanese man sat in small chairs nonchalantly continuing a strange lesson in French."[11] The reviewer goes on to say that the "art was not something that had already been created. It was instead a performance in which the audience, while experiencing the same process with which the performer conducts a seemingly meaningless act before them, was able to gain something."[12]

This description of an event that certainly had many precedents in the Cabaret Voltaire in Zurich towards the end of the First World War, when simultaneous poems were read and dancers emerged from paper wrappings, and artists such as Hans Arp doubled as actors, poets, readers, and painters, reflects the widening conception of theater in Tokyo. The influence of the Theater of the Absurd, particularly Ionesco, was apparent, as it would be in the mid-to-late 1960s in the experimental theater of Kōbō Abe, and after, in 1971, in his own theater group, in which language increasingly gave way to physical gestures and visual effects. For Teshigahara, the primacy of the visual aspects of the events at Sōgetsu, as well as in avant-garde theater experiments elsewhere in Tokyo, was of great interest since he was, at the time, engaged in making films with a pronounced emphasis on the visual impact of his imagery, intended to supersede the word.

In successive events, some in the streets of Tokyo, some in Sōgetsu Hall, many of Teshigahara's contemporaries expressed their disaffection with the entire social organization of Japan, which increasingly seemed corrupt and materialistic, and with the larger industrialist enterprises fattening themselves in the profits of America's war. There were tensions growing amongst the artists themselves and enough pressure from increasingly politicized youth to cause a planned film festival at Sōgetsu in 1969 to be cancelled.

The manner in which the festival was attacked was typical of events in other parts of the world such as the Venice Biennale and the Cannes Film Festival: groups of young people would rush the stage and drown out the proceedings with loud imprecations. At Sōgetsu, it proved impossible to reason with them and impossible to screen the 145 films from general applicants and twenty-seven from invited participants. Sōfū Teshigahara decided to order Hiroshi to cancel the festival. Thus, as Akiyama says, the only place to show films that would never be shown in commercial movie theaters was eliminated.

Teshigahara, who tended to shrink from the more violent expressions of disgust, and whose own work remained disciplined and aesthetically pitched to relatively conventional standards (it would be hard to imagine him condoning, for example, the young Nam June Paik's performance called "Fluxus Champion Contest" in which a ring of men urinate into a bucket while singing their respective national anthems) soon would find his aegis as impresario at Sōgetsu burdensome. His thoughts turned to a new, and for him, totally different film undertaking—a realistic quasi-documentary exploration of a special situation created by the American war in Vietnam. Following attentively the activities of Beheiren, and other groups in the antiwar movement which had begun to work with American soldiers stationed in Japan late in 1967, Teshigahara saw dramatic possibilities in the many questions raised. As Makoto Oda, writing of his experiences, pointed out:

> American soldiers who opposed the war expressed their opposition through a variety of activities ranging from small on-base meetings and the publication of antiwar newspapers to desertion from the front. It was our assistance to those soldiers who had left the front that made us so well known internationally.
>
> We, certainly I personally, were particularly sympathetic toward soldiers who had been sent to Vietnam, for they reminded us of the Japanese soldier who had been sent to China or other places in Asia during Japan's war of aggression. Both conflicts, the Vietnam War and Japan's war of aggression, were unjustifiable conflicts in which ordinary American and Japanese citizens were drafted and sent to the front . . . The draftees were, in general, the victims of the powers above them, which forced them to join the war and to fight. To join the war and to fight meant, in essence, to kill, and in this action, they also became aggressors. The fact was that these soldiers were aggressors precisely *because* they were victims, not *despite* the fact that they were victims. . . . [13]

Teshigahara observed the situation, remarking the countless individual problems it created, and finally decided to make his film, *Summer Soldiers*, collaborating with American script writer, John Nathan. He had not forgotten his critique of Kamei who he thought had "avoided the darker side of issues, the side where contradictions enter." Nor had he forgotten his early admiration of Buñuel's quasi-documentaries in which "people are placed so that the depths of their minds are hinted at effectively." Perhaps it was also around this time that he began to reconsider the work of Ozu, who in earlier years he had rejected for seemingly always making films with "the same old story, the same old patterns and people of the middle class." Eventually, Teshigahara says, "My attitude toward Ozu made a 180-degree change. He really took up the subject of the solitude of human existence by looking at ordinary people from a particular camera angle." Ozu, Teshigahara now says, "didn't make the character tell what he was trying to say. The characters all speak briefly. You came to understand through these remarks seemingly unrelated to each other."

Undoubtedly, the work of the Italian neo-realists revisited his imagination. There is something in his approach in this film that is akin to that of de Sica, who wrote in an article published in 1975 that his purpose in a film such as *The Bicycle Thief* had been "to find the element of drama in daily situations, the marvelous in the news, indeed, in the local news, considered by most people to be worn-out materials."[14]

The film Teshigahara undertook in 1971 required considerable preparations. He and Nathan visited countless people who had taken in the American deserters, interviewed them, assessed their general attitude, and tried to fathom the reasons for the basic failure of the enterprise. He also spoke with American soldiers, some of whom had gone to counseling centers near their base to inquire about ways to resist the war, and others who had made the initial break and had experienced the isolation Teshigahara would depict in the film. Teshigahara told Mellen that he was "most interested in the soldier who deserted for simple reasons at first and was only gradually awakened to political reality, thus becoming aware and sensitive." He resisted the temptation to depict a sophisticated soldier fully committed to "the movement," as the antiwar groupings came to be known.

The problem that had always seemed most significant to Teshigahara—that of communication between people—could be focused poignantly in the film if he included nonprofessional actors who could enter the spirit of the script without preconceptions. The main character, whom Teshigahara went all the way to New York to find, had to be authentically naïve. The New York University student he eventually found, Keith Sykes, appeared visibly immature and played the role of the guitar-playing GI with convincing ingenuousness. *Summer Soldiers*, released in 1972, offered a sober reckoning of the complex issues that arose as the young deserter was passed from family to family and in each case failed to establish rapport. The "element of drama in daily situations" that de Sica had called his essential subject emerged in Teshigahara's film in the way the Japanese couples in various modes of life succumbed to minor irritations with the callow soldier, who responded sullenly or with deliberately boorish behavior. Teshigahara's longstanding views about the ultimately solitary situation of each individual were as apparent in this realistic film as they had been in his previous "metaphysical" films.

He wished to avoid both the sentimentality and oversimplification that bedeviled the peace movement, and to present an aspect of war that few others had considered. In the film, Teshigahara swiftly establishes the situation of the young boy sheltering with an older bar girl near the Iwakumi air base. He shows the boy aimlessly drawing cartoons, listening to country music and starting fearfully each time he hears movements outside. In one scene the Japanese police, accompanied by an American agent, search the room while the woman screams at them that they must have a warrant. One of the few overtly political remarks occurs in the first few minutes of the film when the Japanese policeman apologizes to the woman as he leaves, saying "We do what they want."

Having established the uneasy atmosphere of the hunted and the hunters, Teshigahara then takes the boy on his unhappy peregrination from one Japanese home to another, in the course of which he describes with his camera angles, often in close-ups, the daily life and the cultural mores, ranging from bathing and sleeping habits to food, of the mostly middle class, well-meaning Japanese who took in the fugitive, and of their confused motives. In one scene, for instance, the housewife, seeing his *malhabile* way of handling chopsticks impatiently removes his dish and bones his fish for him. In another, the boy sits in a small, crowded living room with a family, totally isolated, watching a Japanese version of "I Love Lucy." In one of the few touches of surreality, Teshigahara shifts the camera from the lonely boy to a fish tank where the large, gasping face of the fish takes up the whole screen, suggesting his situation. In another scene, Teshigahara's old friend Kanze

Three scenes from Summer Soldiers *(1972); GI deserter (played by Keith Sykes) wandering along the river in Kyoto.*

GI deserter in a Japanese home with husband played by Hideo Kanze.

Young GI deserter playing the guitar.

appears in a traditional Japanese setting—there are even cherry blossoms gently swaying outside the window—with his wife in kimono, whom he urges to go to her mother's house while the fugitive stays with them. The wife demurely asks, "Are these GI's savage?"

Deftly, Teshigahara introduces various Japanese activists, some frightened of the momentous gesture they are about to make, others blindly mouthing their fealty to "the cause," and still others showing, as does a prostitute in a bordello scene, a profound xenophobia. The camera effectively describes each environment, detail by detail, with Teshigahara's habitual precision. There are scenes in Kyoto, where the soldier wanders disconsolately, that provide a sharp contradiction to the usual tourist's view of the lovely old city and scenes at the waterfront where the great apparatus of international shipping overwhelms the slender figure of the boy. Bars, community centers, counseling offices, and the base itself are registered with care, building up the background for the moral issues visually, rather than in the dialogue. Takemitsu's music is extremely spare, used only in linking passages, and never to heighten the drama which Teshigahara is careful to keep as understated as possible, until the brutal climax in the brothel, where "the price is double for a foreigner."

Although the film was meant to raise existential questions rather than to incite political passions, there is one character in the film who is always seen either in close-up, talking to the camera, or jogging with tremendous effort, as the soundtrack suggests by amplifying his heavy breathing. This character plays a Latino deserter who speaks New York street English and berates radicals who don't understand that Che Guevara was "a peaceful man" and who don't take time to read his books. Unlike Jim, the main protagonist, he knows what he is doing and is prepared to take the consequences. He jogs to keep in shape for the work he will undertake as a revolutionary when he finally gets back to "my people." His awareness of the world is in contrast to the blundering innocence of Jim, and it is of considerable interest to read in Mellen's extensive interview with Teshigahara that the filmmaker is most in sympathy with him:

> Mellen: What is the point of view of *Summer Soldiers* toward the American deserters? Is the perception that of the last character in the film who speaks of organizing a revolution?

Teshigahara: I sympathize with the deserters very strongly. But deserting itself doesn't equal opposing the war or the creation of a new, better society. But as a human being, I sympathize with them deeply.

Mellen: Does the director's view equal that of the character in the last shot who is in constant training so that he will be physically fit for the revolution to come?

Teshigahara: Yes, that soldier represents my political point of view more than any other character. But there are various types of deserters . . . [15]

Teshigahara's hopes for the film were not realized financially, although it received several positive reviews. The writer in *Newsweek* magazine, Paul D. Zimmerman, pointed out that there were notably few good movies about the Vietnam War, and Teshigahara's film "sheds a fascinating light on one of the least reported facets of the war."[16] He regarded the film as a "well-balanced view of a delicate situation." Others such as Mellen herself found it uneven and strained. Richard Roud, commenting in his critical dictionary of film, on the other hand, called the film a promising departure from Teshigahara's more metaphysical films. "*Summer Soldiers* was a hard-hitting portrait of a G.I. deserter on the run in Japan and the bar girls and radical leftists who try to help him. Even more surprising, coming from Teshigahara, was the wit of the film when it showed the comic side of the culture clash between the grass-roots, cornfed G.I. and his Japanese hosts."[17]

By the time *Summer Soldiers* was released, Teshigahara's adventure with Sōgetsu Hall had finally come to a close, partly because of financial reasons, and his hopes to make another film faded for the same reason. He was not to undertake another film for seventeen years.

NOTES

1 Kōbō Abe, *World Authors 1950–1970*, 1975, p. 1.

2 Martin Collcutt, "Daimyō and Daimyō Culture," in *Japan, The Shaping of Daimyō Culture*, ed. Yoshiaki Shimizu, Washington, D.C., 1980, p. 10.

3 Thomas Havens, *Fire Across the Sea*, Princeton, 1987.

4 Genpei Akasegawa, "The 1960s. The Art which Destroyed Itself: An Intimate Account," in *Reconstruction: The Role of the Avant-Garde Art in Postwar Japan*, Museum of Modern Art, Oxford, 1985.

5 Akasegawa, *Reconstruction*.

6 Ichirō Hariu, "Progressive Trends in Modern Japanese Art," in *Reconstruction: The Role of the Avant-Garde in Postwar Japan*.

7 Akasegawa, *Reconstruction*.

8 Kaido, *Reconstruction*.

9 John Cage, "On Rauschenberg, Artist and his Work," *Metro*, Vol. I, No. 2, 1961, pp. 36–50.

10 Kuniharu Akiyama, "Yōko Ono: 'FUMIE'," in catalogue for Sōgetsu school, 1990, p. 11.

11 Akiyama, Sōgetsu catalogue.

12 Akiyama, Sōgetsu catalogue.

13 Makoto Oda, "A Writer in the Present World: A Japanese Case History," in *Legacies and Ambiguities: Postwar Fiction and Culture in West Germany and Japan*, Washington, p. 269.

14 "De Sica Su De Sica," *Bianco e Nero*, Sept.–Dec., 1975, p. 259.

15 Mellen, *Voices from the Japanese Cinema*, p. 169.

16 Paul D. Zimmerman, cited in *Cinema: A Critical Dictionary*, ed. Richard Roud, Vol. II, New York, 1979.

17 Zimmerman, *Cinema*.

8

Shortly after *Summer Soldiers* was released, Teshigahara traveled to Fukui Prefecture to scout dramatic backdrops for photographs of his father's sculptures. While exploring the region, he came across the graveyard that his friend, the novelist Tsutomu Mizukami, had called to his attention. There, ancient potters who were too poor to put up tombstones had used large urns which they placed upside down and in which the spirit was supposedly lodged. Teshigahara's curiosity was piqued by these simple and compelling grave markers, and he immediately visited the park in Echizen where there was an experimental ceramic studio.

During this visit he played with clay. This, as he says, was to be a "fateful encounter." With habitual alacrity, he decided on the spot to establish an outpost for Sōgetsu where students, friends, and colleagues could come to experiment with the excellent clay in this ancient pottery enclave. He himself was so entranced with "the earth—but not the pottery art—the *feeling* of clay" that he immediately set to work in Echizen, and by 1974, had produced enough works to have an exhibition.

The region proved to be a powerful antidote to the clutter of Tokyo. Echizen is surrounded by richly forested mountains and many streams. On a clear day, the sea is visible from its heights, and on many other days, the mountains, their flanks dark with evergreen and bamboo growth, are crowned with spectacular clouds. Everything is dramatic, even the weather. When it is hot, Teshigahara says, it is not simply hot but *very* hot, and when it is cold, it is freezing. He quickly adapted to

Teshigahara and assistants with one of his large pots at Takashimaya Department Store, November 1981.

these extremes, which would find expression in the increasingly large and eccentric pots he produced there.

Echizen offered a retreat, a respite from the pressures of urban life, and still today draws Teshigahara back regularly. But his turning to ceramics had a prehistory. As a youth he had attentively followed the activities of his father's friend, Isamu Noguchi. One of Noguchi's many undertakings in Japan was his intensive study of traditional Japanese ceramic art. He spent months in Kamakura as a friend and student of the renowned unconventional potter, Rosanjin Kitaōji (1883–1959). Rosanjin, known as a difficult and highly eccentric man, as a youth had called himself *doppo*, or "lone wolf," and his course as an artist in clay was consistent with that vision of himself. Noguchi, given the run of Rosanjin's kiln, and the choice of the many clays Rosanjin stored in his Kamakura studio, set to work to produce sculptures and vessels in which all the cultures he had studied, above all ancient Japanese, were reflected. The simple works, fashioned from slabs of clay and mostly unglazed, astonished the artists who came to the Kanazawa Prefectural Museum of Modern Art in 1952 to see what the famous American artist had done in Japan. Many of the younger artists were obdurately hostile to anachronisms in Noguchi's work; but Teshigahara, who early recognized Noguchi as a master of form, remembered, and when the time came, set out, as had Noguchi, to work with clay as a creative artist rather than as a potter.

In addition to Noguchi's pervasive influence, there was that of Teshigahara's mentor, Okamoto, who had begun to talk about prehistoric Japanese art in the 1950s. Okamoto, whose expertise as a Sorbonne graduate in ethnology lent him authority, was one of several important figures in Japan who turned their attention to the Jōmon culture. No doubt Okamoto's experience in Paris, when the people he consorted with, among them Georges Bataille and André Breton, were seeking inspiration in the oldest cultures they could identify, had stimulated his interest in his own traditions.

Artists and scholars, in the period between the world wars all over the Western world, were searching ancient horizons for alternative views of the world. The tremendous interest in so-called primitive art was spurred by the desire to transcend the limitations imposed by increasing nationalism in twentieth-century societies. In France, artists looked to the traditional societies of Africa (particularly in the French colonies) for alternative world views, while in the United States, artists became interested in Native American traditions, particularly on the northwest coast, where they studied various Indian tribes through their artifacts and architecture. In Japan, naturally enough, intellectuals turned their attention to the earliest artifacts they could find—those of the Jōmon culture. Archaeologists after the Second World War were busy excavating many prehistoric sites, and by the 1960s, there was a considerable literature on the mysterious peoples of the Jōmon era.

Certainly, one of the attractive aspects of the Jōmon study was the light it shed on the issue of nationality. Many scholars had suggested that the Jōmon people were a mixture of migrants from Siberia and southern China. The intellectuals who turned their attention to the exceptional ceramic sculpture left by the Jōmon culture were often in full rebellion against the mythology of the emperor system. They were eager to find the kind of international syncretism Jōmon undoubtedly represented, while yet recognizing its unique aesthetic qualities germane

Helmet *by Isamu Noguchi, 1952. Ceramic, 71.5 x 33 x 31.5 cm. Sōgetsu Museum.*

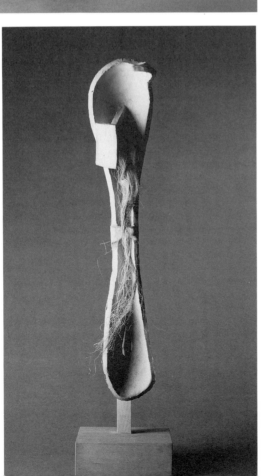

Sunflower *by Isamu Noguchi, 1952. Ceramic with wooden base, 65 x 34 x 18.5 cm. Sōgetsu Museum.*

Ghost *by Isamu Noguchi, 1952. Ceramic and hemp with wooden base, 86.5 x 19.9 x 19.6 cm. Sōgetsu Museum.*

to the Japanese islands. Recent scholarship bears out earlier speculations. A description by a current scholar says the people were physically and ethnically diverse:

> Crossing land bridges and spreading throughout the islands, the earliest human populations apparently came to Japan from eastern and southeastern Asia near the end of the Pleistocene era, by at least thirty thousand years ago. Around fourteen thousand years ago, populations from northeastern Asia migrated to Japan via Hokkaidō; during the Jōmon period Mongoloid populations apparently came to Japan from Neolithic and Bronze Age cultures and from northeastern Asia. Intensive rice cultivating people also entered western Japan from Korea around 400 B.C.[1]

The writer adds that, "The Jōmon tradition of low-fired ceramics, which entails a preference for earthy colors, rich textures, and surface effects, seems to be preserved in Japanese aesthetics as a parallel to the more formal, symmetrical shapes and regular decorative patterns that often came from the Asian continent."[2]

The extraordinary "flame style" pots discovered in the twentieth century impressed certain Japanese artists who could identify this exuberant impulse, with its baroque asymmetry and uninhibited manipulation of leathery clay, with their own revolt against traditional Japanese refinement. Teshigahara's generation was not only alerted to the special qualities of the oldest Japanese ceramic tradition by Okamoto, but also by the architect Kenzo Tange, who in 1964, wrote his book about Ise, in which he said:

> I hold the view that there have been two strains within Japanese culture, the Jōmon and the Yayoi, the vital and the aesthetic, and that the cultural development has been the history of their interplay.[3]

Noguchi, who had discussed this issue for many years with Tange, remarked later, "All my friends from Tange to Teshigahara always talk of themselves as being Jōmon and not Yayoi, Yayoi being the first evidence of the sort of refinement the Japanese are capable of."[4]

Around the time Teshigahara was establishing the Sōgetsu kiln in Echizen, Noguchi was establishing his Japanese studio in Mure in Shikoku. He soon visited his friend in his new studio in Echizen and was startled by Teshigahara's sculptured works:

> Finally there came a day when I was invited to go to Echizen in Fukui where Hiroshi, it seemed, wished to establish a pottery kiln using the once famous earth of the locality. This was no doubt to help with flowers but nevertheless an improbable project.[5]

Noguchi praised Teshigahara's "earthenwares of extreme originality and anguish of form."[6] The often contorted forms were typical of Teshigahara's ceramic works from the beginning. He described his early experience in Echizen by saying, "I had a childlike pleasure in making any shape I pleased out of clay, seeing it baked, and encountering the unexpected result. My instinctive urge for plastic creation was evoked by clay . . . I didn't use a potter's wheel because I wanted to freely express my own feelings in plastic art, not aiming at a refined pot or a stable structure."[7]

Teshigahara's most attentive critic in the area of ceramics, Yoshiaki Inui, quotes Teshigahara in what he calls "an interesting remark":

> Things made of clay are easily broken. When the piece is on the point of being broken and yet retains its integrity—this is the point at which it is beautiful. Regular artisans try to avoid that extremity and aim at achieving perfect stability. But I do not. I aim to bring the work to the most dangerous, unstable point . . . [8]

This "interesting remark" is not an expression of humility. It is not simply the use of humble clay that inspired Teshigahara, but his love of paradox—the innate rebelliousness that made him respond to Okamoto's theory of extreme contrasts, and to the various attempts, on the part of avant-garde members of his own generation, to flout what they regarded as over-civilized, tired traditions. In the rough surfaces and imperfect profiles of his earliest ceramic works, Teshigahara declared himself: it was not so much love of *sabi*—the old, the crumbling, the cracked, the imperfect—as the force of his desire to break out, to express direct intuitions unmediated by tuition or tradition. Using the clay of Echizen with its high iron content in which, as Inui says, "the rough shiny black surface conveys the essence of clay's tactility . . . a type of beauty expressive of heaviness, dynamic power, and fortitude,"[9] Teshigahara was able to satisfy his instinctive desire for the unregimented expression that derives directly from the universal and fundamental creative drive.

From his earliest experiments, Teshigahara twisted and squeezed, scored and tore the clay as the spirit moved him. Pots were asymmetrical with tubes protruding or handles pulled out in unlikely places, and frequently, the natural luster of the fired clay was left unadorned. For him, glazes were a source of further experimentation, and he often used unorthodox methods to achieve strange juxtapositions of color and reflecting light. Sometimes his surfaces were scored with whatever instrument came to hand, as simply the rope-incised decoration of the earliest Jōmon potters. Teshigahara was not preoccupied with restoring the art of pottery, as was the movement in Japan in the twentieth century that sought to reinvigorate folk traditions, nor was he concerned with the stylistic impress of the master artist. In his recourse to clay, Teshigahara seemed, at least in the early stages, to want to achieve a kind of suspended existence in which the act of shaping clay would release his deepest urges, would assuage his thirst for an immediate action with no precedents in mind.

What the men of his father's generation, such as Tange, Noguchi, and Sōfū himself, had sought when they championed Jōmon over Yayoi was to free themselves from the great body of laws that had encumbered one side of Japanese art history and to reinstate an alternate tradition that had always been present from prehistoric times. Despite their commitment to modern art, all of Sōfū's friends had felt the need to buttress their tendencies with references to tradition (as finally all vanguardists do). Already in the 1920s and 1930s, the most advanced artists, particularly those who traveled to the great European centers, had attempted to find precedents in Japanese traditions for their modern tastes. Most often, they looked to the period in which Zen Buddhism took root. If they were poets, they saw correlations between haiku and Surrealist imagery. If they were painters or sculptors, they sought the calligraphy and painting of the Zen monks who were least affected by the conventions passed down by previous generations.

Echizen kiln, 1980.

Obviously the Zen emphasis on process rather than product had a great appeal to the first Surrealist generation after the war, when the whole world seemed intent on stressing informal, spontaneous impulses. All throughout the postwar period there were allusions to the power of the unconscious, to the merit of the swiftly remarked emotion, to the importance of intuition over the rational mind. But it was not until after the chaos of the Vietnam War period that younger artists openly sought precedents for their acts in the traditions of various Japanese art forms.

*Large ash-glazed ceramic sculpture
by Teshigahara, 1980. Stoneware,
52 x 138 x 61 cm.*

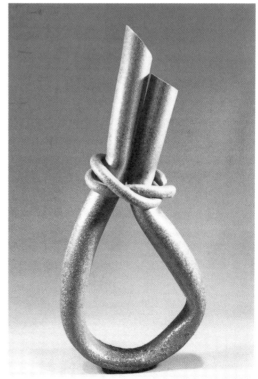

*Ceramic by Teshigahara, 1978.
Stoneware, 81.5 x 35.5 x 15 cm.*

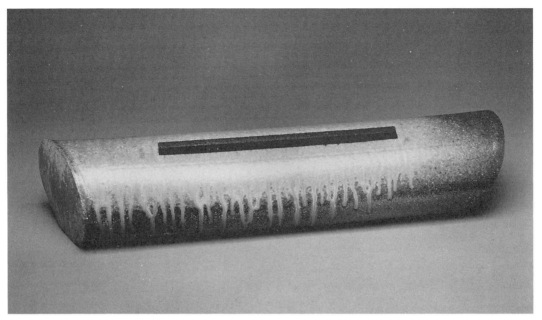

Ash-glazed flower container by Teshigahara. Stoneware, 14 x 61 x 15 cm.

Flower vase by Teshigahara, 1982.
Stoneware, 62.5 x 31 x 20.5 cm.

Flower vase by Teshigahara, 1990.
Stoneware, 61.9 x 51 x 44 cm.

Teshigahara himself was not interested in academic scholarship. But he, like many of his peers, in the course of following his impulses, inevitably encountered the tradition most congenial to his temperament. It is as if he and his friends were consciously following the advice of Bashō who, in his farewell words to Kyoraku in 1693, wrote:

> Do not seek to follow in the footsteps of men of old; seek what they sought. That is what Kūkai wrote . . . [10]

What Kūkai actually wrote was:

> In writing poetry a study of the old forms is an excellent thing, but it is no mark of ability to copy old poems. In calligraphy too, it is good to imitate the old conceptions, but it is not a mark of skill to make one's writings resemble the old examples.[11]

Increasingly, the oldest sources of Japanese aesthetics were reconsidered by the postwar generation and served to ratify their own inclinations. The writings of Kūkai (Kōbō Daishi, 774–835) were resurrected and his paradoxes savored, as when he wrote that, "The law of Buddha is not based on the word, but without the word cannot reveal itself in its plenitude," or, "The Ultimate Reality is totally free of forms and colors, but it is in forms and colors that it can be seized."[12] Kūkai's repeated assertion that he penetrated his studies with both instinct and reason would later give way, during the Muromachi period, to an increasingly exclusive emphasis on instinct among many of the most prominent artists. The great painter Sesshū, for example, repeatedly declared his independence from received ideas about the nature of his art, and in his old age wrote: "And I, when my sight is already weak and I have attained an advanced age . . . I still don't know the why and how of my work."[13]

Not knowing the why and how became a point of pride for the postwar generation as it plunged into the extravagant vanguard activities of the 1960s. Intermittently, Abe, Takemitsu, Teshigahara, and others scoured the past for precedents. Among others they discovered Yoshida Kenkō (1283–1350), who never bothered to gather his thoughts in a formal presentation but left scraps of paper pinned to his wall. These

Winter Landscape *(left) and* Autumn Landscape *by Sesshū Tōyō. Pair of hanging scrolls, ink on paper, each 46.3 x 29.3 cm. Tokyo National Museum.*

would be gathered only much later, in 1431. Kenkō's philosophic stance—"Truly, the beauty in life is its uncertainty"—tinctured his aesthetic which, as he wrote, cherished the fragmentary over the whole, the worn over the new. "Whatever the object, its perfection is a fault. Leave things unfinished."[14]

During the same period, Musō Soseki, whose thoughts were highly esteemed and cited by Noguchi, proffered a philosophy of art that exalted the power of intuition. His disdain for "words and phrases" suited the mood of artists in modern Japan.

From Kenkō to Rikyū, who would soon preoccupy Teshigahara, was an obvious transition that more than a few artists by the 1930s were willing to make. Teshigahara arrived little by little, first tasting the pleasures of clay, and then seriously taking up the calligraphers's brush. This,

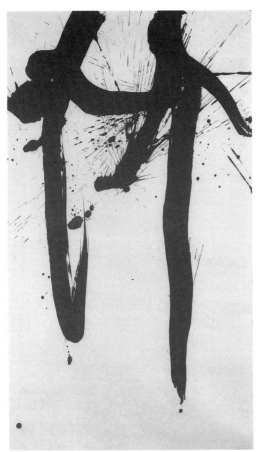

Three versions of the charac-
ter for "bamboo" ("take")
by Teshigahara, 1987–89.
Ink on paper, 197 x 108
cm./183.2 x 93 cm.

Koan no Eki *by Georges Mathieu, 1957. Oil on canvas, 200 x 800 cm. Sōgetsu Museum.*

too, was attributed to an accidental encounter in Echizen, although Teshigahara concedes that Sōfū's radical calligraphy had deeply impressed him during the trip to Europe. In Echizen, he found a small industry near his village devoted to the making of fine papers. With so many types of paper readily available, Teshigahara took to his brush, inventing his own calligraphic style (which he insists is not a style at all but an expression). He did not seek models from the past, nor was he methodical in his choice of poetry to indite. Once Teshigahara began, his own practice lured him to notice exceptional figures in the history of calligraphy.

Almost invariably Teshigahara was drawn to the nonconformists, among them Musō Soseki. Noguchi was constantly citing the Japanese sage who had mastered the arts of the Sung period without ever going to China, and who had practiced the arts of the calligrapher, poet, and composer of gardens. Musō, who in his old age signed himself "the simple and artless old man," lent force to Zen principles in calligraphy by insisting that the power of the brush could capture a kind of truth not available to the rational mind.

Musō was one of several singular figures in the history of Japanese calligraphy who attracted Teshigahara, who had a natural affinity for those who had managed to set out on their own course, purposefully avoiding precedents. He was repeatedly drawn to the foyers of those in the past who had followed their bent and were eccentric to central traditions.

Among his enthusiasms, predictably, is the remarkable Ikkyū Sōjun (1394–1481), who claimed he was a son of the emperor Go-Komatsu by a woman of low rank who had been banished from the palace. As a youth, Ikkyū had been a disciple of a monk who had left the important Kyoto temple complex of Daitokuji to become a hermit on the shores of Lake Biwa. In a celebrated conversion story, Ikkyū achieved *satori* while floating on the lake, which seemed to have freed him from all social constraints. He was the subject of countless stories of scandalous behavior. By his own proud admission, he was a frequenter of taverns and brothels during his sojourn at the seaport of Sakai:

> I sing an ordinary, dirty song of wine-lust,
> woman-lust, poetry, and plain lust.[15]

Despite his unseemly behavior, Ikkyū eventually became the chief priest of a sub-temple at Daitokuji, but he did not last long. In 1440, he abruptly resigned, leaving a poem for the abbot denouncing the red tape of the organization of the large monastery, and adding, "If some-day you want to look me up, try the fish shop, the tavern, or the brothel." His poetry casts aspersions on orthodox blockheads who scarcely knew their Zen and revels in shocking announcements of his own freedom and Zen sagacity, after his "ten years in the brothels—hard to wear out desire." His underlying commitment, however, is never forgotten:

> Contemplating the Law, reading sutras, trying to be a real master;
> yellow robes, the stick, the shouts, till my wooden seat's all crooked;
> but it seems my real business was always in the muck,
> with my great passion for women, and for boys as well.[16]

Ikkyū's calligraphy reflects his gusto, his "plain lust." He often worked with a stiff brush in mixed cursive and semi-cursive modes, swiftly laying down swirling strokes with pronounced diagonals until the brush went dry. Ikkyū, among other singular Japanese calligraphers and poets, was striv-ing for the quality Chinese calligraphers called *chi'i*, sometimes trans-lated as "inner force." Difficult to define, the concept of *chi'i*, according to the scholar, Yu-kung Kao, can be found in calligraphy in several layers:

> On the level of physical action, *chi'i* is translatable as "kinetic force," which determines the bodily movement in the execu-tion of writing. On the level of mental action, it is "intentional force" which directs the artist to fulfill his plan. But between these two ends one can also conceive of different frames of reference, such as the "pulsatile force" or "impulsive force" as

Calligraphy by Ikkyū Sōjun. Pair of hanging scrolls, ink on paper, each 133.3 x 41.8 cm. Shinjuan, Daitokuji.

the momentum moves upward from the physiological level to the intellectual level. Ultimately, on the highest interpretive level, all these forces join as "life force," to symbolize the personality as a whole. One must not forget that precisely this same *chi'i* is, in metaphysics, the "cosmic force" that informs the structure of all nature, including certainly the writing medium itself. It seems a natural step to use this calligraphical form to represent the different levels of interpretations for this inner force. The stark contrast between black ink and white background is the simplest metaphor for the forces of nature; the movement of this force only minimally defined by a linear course with infinite possible variations in amplitude and direction.[17]

Teshigahara's preference for the literati painters, whose calligraphy often signalled their unwillingness to be entrapped by sheer technique, and who wanted, he says, "to break through and express themselves freely," is consistent with his earliest views of the function of an artist. He did not forswear the visible meaning in Chinese characters as did some of his peers in the 1950s, who practiced an expressionist, non-literal calligraphy that they tried to align with Western postwar painting tendencies. But, he also did not wish to be enslaved by the enormous literature on calligraphy with its endless instructions and minute codifications of every stroke. In both his ceramic experimentation and calligraphy, Teshigahara extended Okamoto's theory of contrasting, even conflicting modes, seeking, as he has so often said, the most perilous of paths.

NOTES

1   *Ancient Japan*, ed. Richard Pearson, Washington, D.C., 1992, p. 63.

2   Ibid., p. 74.

3   Kenzō Tange, *Ise Prototype of Japanese Architecture*, Boston, 1965.

4   Dore Ashton, *Noguchi East and West*, New York, 1992, p. 201.

5   Isamu Noguchi, in *Hiroshi Teshigahara*, Tokyo, 1983, p. 7.

6   Noguchi, ibid., p. 7.

7   Teshigahara, *Furuta Oribe*.

8   Yoshiaki Inui in *Hiroshi Teshigahara: Works 1978–1987*, Tokyo, 1987, p. 255.

9   Inui in *Hiroshi Teshigahara*.

10 Bashō, *Sources of Japanese Tradition*, p. 446.

11 Kūkai, ibid., p. 38.

12 Kūkai, ibid., p. 38.

13 Sesshū, ibid., p. 152.

14 Kenkō, ibid., p. 190.

15 Ikkyū Sōjun, *Kodansha Encyclopedia of Japan*, Tokyo, 1983, vol. 3, pp. 269–70.

16 Ikkyū, ibid.

17 Yu-king Kao, "Chinese Lyrical Aesthetics," in *Words and Images*, ed. Alfreda Murck and W.C. Fong, Princeton, 1991, p. 78.

*D*uring the Second World War, the art of ikebana, despite its innocuous function, did not flourish. Aside from the fact that there were no flowers to arrange since all the flower fields had been turned into potato fields, as Teshigahara remarks, almost all those in the artistic professions were impressed as propagandists. Teshigahara's father was no exception and was sent to China.

After the war, during the first dreadful months, the family was evacuated to the countryside of Gunma Prefecture. One day a Government Headquarters jeep drew up to the house, and Sōfū was alarmed. "He thought they had finally come to get us," Teshigahara recalls, as they had certain artists regarded as collaborators. Instead, it was an invitation to teach ikebana to the wives of American officers in Tokyo.

So began the spectacular postwar development of Sōfū's Sōgetsu School that eventually counted hundreds of thousands of students and graduates. By around 1974, Sōfū was in the unusual position to ask his old friend Kenzō Tange to design a new building to house the world headquarters on a choice site overlooking the Imperial gardens. Between 1974 and 1977, Tange built a skyscraper clad in blue mirror glass to catch the light of the seasons. The building housed a museum, restaurant, offices, classrooms, several Japanese-style rooms, and a dramatic lobby for which Tange enlisted the services of Noguchi to create a sculptured stone garden and exhibition space. In addition, there was a large, well-equipped auditorium for which Hiroshi designed ceramic panels. Sōfū confidently assumed the duties this huge enterprise demanded, but within two years, in September 1979, he died. Long before, he had begun to prepare his daughter Kasumi to inherit the title of *iemoto*, but in an unexpected tragedy, she died soon after her father.

Teshigahara was profoundly shaken by the two deaths and perplexed to think that he could become the third *iemoto*. He realized, as he said in an interview, that he was left with two choices:

> To succeed to the school and become the third *iemoto*, or just let the school go. I was very distressed. I never expected to lead such a huge organization. Although I . . . was accustomed to seeing my father's work, I was not a specialized ikebana artist. . . . I was troubled by the paradox of being an experimental artist and a son of the *iemoto* at the same time, but consciously or unconsciously, I had always been helped as part of Sōgetsu . . . [1]

What Teshigahara called the "paradox" was, in fact, a contradiction that he eventually chose to live with, often with ambivalent feelings. The very structure of ikebana schools contradicted the ideals of the postwar avant-garde, and especially Okamoto, who had written passionately against the old feudal hierarchies, guilds, and apprentice systems. Like other organizations devoted to traditional arts such as Noh theater or tea ceremony, ikebana schools are structured on the pyramid principle.

In countless attacks, artists of Teshigahara's generation had excoriated what they always referred to as the pyramid principle that, together with the emperor system, seemed to them inconsistent with both their aesthetic and political ideals. The progressive spirits with whom Teshigahara had associated during his college days were implacable opponents to the vertical hierarchies of the past even in their somewhat modified forms found in cultural pursuits after the Meiji restoration. Nothing exemplified the residue of archaic authoritarian structures more than the *iemoto* system which vested absolute authority in the single figure of the director of the school.

During the Meiji period, it is true, there were subtle alterations, but they only led to other objectionable developments, such as the commercialization of the system, as Michio Hayashi has pointed out. Teshigahara's critical friends were all too aware of this unwelcome development in the ancient system. Another deplorable development during the Meiji period, Hayashi says, is the strong emphasis on "Japaneseness" which obviously went counter to the internationalist ambitions of both Teshigahara and his artistic colleagues. Generally speaking, Teshigahara's generation of intellectuals regarded the emperor system ushered in during the Meiji era as inherently incompatible with the open society they advocated, and as Hayashi observes, considered that "any traditional cultural institution with the pyramidal system of organization had its psychological, if not cultural roots, in the emperor system."[3]

For Teshigahara to become *iemoto* meant risking his status as an independent, progressive figure in the modern Japanese cultural landscape. Many of his friends and associates warned him or urged him to let it all go. Certain close friends, such as Arata Isozaki, noticed the effect of a personal crisis in Teshigahara after his father's death, and commented:

> Teshigahara himself seems to be experiencing the metamorphosis that he related in the 1966 picture *The Face of Another* in which the hero, who wears a mask, transforms his own personality. While wearing the outward mask of the *iemoto*, Teshigahara is projecting on himself and the image of his work the metamorphosis that has long been the object of his pursuit.[4]

There were many considerations for Teshigahara, not the least that a great many people depended on the Sōgetsu School for their livelihoods. But it was probably the powerful personality of Sōfū, who had managed to be both the authority figure in a traditional manner and a forceful and recognized member of the avant-garde, that most affected Teshigahara's decision. All his life Teshigahara had been aware that his father defied tradition in countless ways, most particularly in the art of ikebana. He was all too aware of Sōfū's dynamic personality and had struggled in his youth to find an identity of his own. Sōfū, built like a barrel, with a large-featured head and decisive gestures, was a charismatic figure. He held on to the prerogatives of the *iemoto* even as he forged ahead in his career as an avant-garde sculptor. When he first exhibited in New York at the Martha Jackson Gallery, for example, he entered the opening majestically, with his retinue at his heels, and extracted even from the American artists the behavior of respectful disciples, at least on the occasion.

It was not only duty that attached Teshigahara to his father. He had always respected his father's undertakings, and as early as 1952, while he was actively engaged with radical political groups, he had taken time to co-edit Sōfū's book on ikebana. At that time, the number of Sōgetsu followers was estimated to be more than 40,000. An admirer writing the preface stressed the two "mottoes" of Sōfū's regime: "Continue fresh creations. Set styles must be avoided," and "Always look forward to a fresh and vivid world and do not become buried in retrospection." It would prove difficult for a son, even a rebellious son, to renounce these principles, and in fact, similar attitudes are taught to this day at Sōgetsu. Even then, the writer, Sumio Mizusawa, could speak of the "paradox" in Sōfū's "status as a modern exponent of a formative art and his position as a leader of a 'school' which though becoming modernized still carries with it many trends of the past," the very paradox Hiroshi inherited.[5] Sōfū's point of view, which he broadcast widely in books and in the house magazine circulated throughout the world, was always strong and sometimes blunt, as when, in his book, *The Boundless World of Flowers and Form* (1966), he pronounced that:

> The reason why we can love flowers and still sacrifice them in the pursuit of ikebana is the same as the reason why we love animals but still eat meat. Namely, it is a question of necessity. Ikebana is a preordained drama played out between man and flowers.[6]

This drama, which had never commanded Hiroshi's loyalties, would become intelligible to him only when he was forced to be a featured player. Sōfū's notable flexibility made it fairly difficult to reject his views. Hiroko Narasaki, who once edited *Sōgetsu* magazine, demonstrated Sōfū's indomitable adventurousness when she recalled Robert Rauschenberg's visits to Sōgetsu:

> When Rauschenberg did a demonstration at Sōgetsu, he asked for a *kinbyōbu*, a gold-leafed folding screen, so Sōfū ordered a bright gold folding screen of the best quality. While we watched what he was going to do with the screen, he suddenly tore it dramatically. Everybody there was astonished; they also knew the screen was costly. We expected Sōfū would be very angry, but on the contrary, he kept perfect composure

Robert Rauschenberg creating Gold Standard *at Sōgetsu Hall, 1964. Sōgetsu Museum Collection.*

and told us to calm down. Rauschenberg placed the dog character of HMV on it and hooked the chain to the tear in the screen . . . We were so frightened we kept watching Sōfū's face instead of the demonstration. He said, "Well, it is interesting, don't make a fuss. I made a perfect screen but he cannot do anything if he doesn't break it."[7]

Hiroshi himself had to symbolically break through Sōfū's gilded screen. When he assumed the role of *iemoto* in 1980, he seemed to have thrown himself into the task with marked zeal. He studiously reconsidered the art of ikebana and the way pioneered by Sōfū, concentrating on the three-dimensional possibilities inherent in flower arranging. "I have cut away anything which connects the materials to the superficial idea of nature," he wrote. "To do that I have to take away the name of each individual material and treat each as a substance . . . not imitating nature but creating what is unique . . . When the object is merely a substance then it has potential for ikebana."[8] By releasing plant material from its natural associations, Teshigahara gradually asserted himself as a creative artist, wielding form, mass, and line first as a draftsman, next as a sculptor, and finally as a creator of both environmental and interior installations that would, once he discovered the plasticity of bamboo, become his major activity as an ikebana artist.

Among other duties expected of the *iemoto*, there were the events called demonstrations. These he undertook with enthusiasm since they exacted from him something of the skill of a movie director and actor—roles with which he was more than familiar. During the first few years of his life as *iemoto*, Teshigahara traveled the world—Singapore, India, Paris, England, and Russia—demonstrating ikebana. In addition, in 1981, he held an exhibition in Paris where he exhibited at L'Espace Pierre Cardin a number of his compositions of tough, entwining vines and roots, played against the irregular volumes of his large pots. Even here, Teshigahara's necessary confrontation with the ephemeral nature of the art of ikebana was marked, and several reviewers spoke of the principle of metamorphosis at the heart of his expression.

Teshigahara's own remarks about the "impromptu performance" of demonstrations announce developments to come. He speaks of being aware of the attention of an audience which conveys to the demonstrator, "a keenly physical sensation from the materials with which he is involved":

> Aware that nothing will remain of his ikebana at the end, he
> is torn, as he works, between the rival perceptions of spectator
> and maker. The climax toward which he ascends is a momen-
> tary yet dramatic one.[9]

Still, the climax in demonstrations could not satisfy Teshigahara, whose anterior life as a visual artist had been so rich and varied. Casting about for a means to transcend the classical gestures of the flower arranger, he discovered a "substance that stimulated his imagination and offered the possibilities of expansion that he required." In 1982, Teshigahara began his long romance with bamboo, an infinitely flexible material that nevertheless required great invention to bend it to his will. Moving out from the *tokonoma* to the room to the unlimited spaces existing outside the frame of the house, was essential.

His first important outdoor work with bamboo combined both calligraphy and ikebana in a new form. At the Shiseido Art House, Teshigahara installed a host of split bamboo forms that were inverted. The linear shapes could be read as the Chinese character *hito*, which means "person." Soon after, Teshigahara installed another large group of split bamboos in a pond in front of the open air theater in Togamura. This time the bamboo, installed in water, floated upward and, in the beautiful linear arcs of its split members, suggested weeping willows.

These works were Teshigahara's entry into the field of what had come to be called "environmental art," and what Professor Inui calls quite simply, "gardens." With these experiences, Teshigahara was well prepared to undertake a garden assignment offered by the architect Yoshio Taniguchi, who had been asked to design a museum in Sakata for the storage and exhibition of some seventy thousand works willed to his hometown by the photographer Ken Domon.

With rare deference, Taniguchi had invited the sculptor Isamu Noguchi to contribute his thoughts from the outset of the project. Teshigahara, now a close friend of Noguchi, shared in discussions and developed his idea for the garden in the rear of the museum in the collaborative spirit he had always advocated.

Taniguchi asked Teshigahara to address himself to a specific problem: "I told him I needed something like glue between my building and the environment." Teshigahara assessed the site—a park surrounded by rice fields beneath a small mountain—in which Taniguchi had planned a discreet, angular building to contrast with the flowing lines of the landscape.

Teshigahara's design was as muted and calm as the spirit of Taniguchi's building, revealing one side of his nature. This was not the flamboyant, expressionist style in which he had worked as a ceramic sculptor, or even the baroque manner in which he had arranged tough roots and vines in his initial experiments in ikebana. Rather, this garden was reticent, subtle. Teshigahara had, by this time, begun to think seriously about the past of Japan, and clearly he had pondered the meanings and effects of the traditional Zen gardens. His creation for Ken Domon was a homage to the creators of both the dry landscape garden and the stroll garden. He formed an echo to the pond on which the museum seems to float at the front entrance in the dry bed of riverstones curving around toward the slope behind. He planted dwarf bamboo to accent the sinuous curves of his design that appear to merge with the graded hill behind. Pacing out the spaces, Teshigahara installed a few larger stones at intervals to induce the illusion of amplification of the space, which relates to the natural hill beyond.

This thoughtful design was dependent on Teshigahara's feeling for the kind of space Taniguchi envisioned: one like the old Zen enclaves in which the verandas facing the gardens were at once part of the building itself and openings to nature. Within the museum today, visitors can sit before the large veranda-like window facing Teshigahara's backdrop to the building and experience the softly flowing composition in much the same way they might experience a Kyoto garden. Teshigahara had at last been able to reconcile the aesthetic of the Japanese past with his modern impulse. Thereafter, it would no longer be difficult for him to read the meaning of his presence in the twentieth century through the past, at least partially.

His new freedom concerning the past made it possible for him to seek opportunities to implant his radical notion of ikebana in the most traditional settings. Several times during the 1980s, he repaired to ancient sites—temples in Kyoto and elsewhere—where he introduced his unorthodox environmental ideas of ikebana with considerable success. What had once seemed unthinkable—the resurrection of great Japanese aesthetic traditions—was now a natural way, and Teshigahara would soon embark on a grand project inspired by his attention to the remarkable Muromachi and Momoyama periods.

NOTES

1   Conversation between Shōji Okauchi and Hiroshi Teshigahara, in *Zen'ei-Chou-Sho*, Japan, 1989.

2   Nakane Chie, *Japanese Society*, Berkeley, 1970, p. 58 and Ann Waswo, *Japanese Landlords*, Berkeley, 1977, pp. 29–30.

3   Michio Hayashi, art historian, professor, and critic, in a letter to the author

4   Arata Isozaki.

5   Sōfū Teshigahara, *Ikebana*, introduction by Sumio Mizusawa, ed. Hiroshi Teshigahara and Koen Shigemori, Tokyo, 1952, p. 24.

6   Sōfū Teshigahara, *This Boundless World of Flowers and Form*, Tokyo, 1966, p. 104.

7   *Sōfū's Eyes*, excerpt from a conversation with Hiroshi Teshigahara, Isamu Noguchi and Ouko Narazaki, Kyoto, 1981.

8   Cited by Yoshiaki Inui in *Hiroshi Teshigahara Works 1978–1987*, Tokyo, 1987, p. 257.

9   Hiroshi Teshigahara, *Transfiguration and Composition*, Tokyo, 1985, p. 13.

10

Reconsiderations of Japanese traditions surfaced sporadically throughout the postwar period. As early as the 1950s, Takemitsu had turned his attention to *gagaku* and the music of the Noh theater, studying "the similarities and divergences between the spatial and temporal structure of Noh and the music of Webern."[1] By the early 1960s, Takemitsu had begun to combine Western orchestral instruments with traditional Japanese instruments such as the *shakuhachi* and the *biwa*. Isozaki, perhaps inspired by his mentor, Tange, who had published a study of the ancient Shintō shrine at Ise in 1964, immersed himself in the consideration of the old Japanese concept, *ma*, and eventually organized the extraordinary exhibition, *Ma: Space/Time in Japan*, in Paris in 1978. Many young French artists were enthralled with the exhibition, and certain luminaries, such as Jacques Derrida and Michel Foucault, sought out Isozaki for searching discussions. As Isozaki points out, the French intellectuals were all familiar with the writings of Daisetz Suzuki, and also, by that time, Tanizaki's moving tribute to the old ways, *In Praise of Shadows*, had been translated.

Teshigahara's turn toward the Japanese past, however, had little in common with the stance of older figures of Sōfū's generation such as Tanizaki and Kawabata and the younger Mishima. The plaintive nostalgia in Kawabata's work—he had said after the war that henceforth he would write nothing but elegies—was rejected by Teshigahara and his colleagues. Kawabata's melancholic longing for an idealized past was seen as sentimental. He seemed to resent both Western interest in

Japanese tradition and Japanese attraction to Western art. In *The Old Capital* he testily observed that André Malraux had made "world famous" Shigemori and Minamoto's portraits in his museum without walls. He faintly mocked his heroine's attention to Klee and Chagall, and noted with regret that her parents, although they still slept on futons, used an electric blanket.

Teshigahara and his friends, on the contrary, turned back to selected traditions in the past to mine them for their living possibilities. They emphatically rejected elegiac nostalgia of the kind captured so well by the filmmaker Ozu, whose sad characters, dispossessed of their familiar prewar world, sit disconsolately in bars and sing old army songs. What Teshigahara sought to do was to unearth a usable past, as Noguchi had long advised him to do.

Noguchi's promptings had not always met with approval in Japan, but gradually his admirers among the younger artists such as Takemitsu, Taniguchi, and Teshigahara shared his vision during his last years, when he set out to demonstrate through his works the sum of his convictions. They now considered it acceptable to highlight exceptional figures in the past who in some way behaved in an unconventional manner or had invigorated Japanese art by breaking hallowed traditions.

Noguchi had been keenly aware of the genius of certain past masters ever since his tour of ancient Japan with Saburō Hasegawa in 1950. For years he had exhorted his Japanese colleagues to think about them, study their works, and consider what they had in common with the Western modernists. He had spoken of his great interest in Sen no Rikyū (1522–1591), whom he had first discovered in the best-selling English edition of Okakura's *Book of Tea*, and later, in Suzuki's books on Zen. Noguchi saw Rikyū as a kindred spirit. Since he himself was steeped in the modernist's vision of the total work of art, Noguchi could easily translate Rikyū's remarkable undertakings into modern terms. Wagner's notion of the *Gesamtkunstwerk* had formed a powerful undercurrent in the Western avant-garde, as Noguchi knew. It had been thoroughly examined in the Russian revolutionary period by such artists as Kandinsky and El Lissitsky, in Germany in the Bauhaus, and in Paris in the theater. Moreover, Noguchi's own most powerful influence from the Rumanian sculptor Brancusi was based as much on the implications of Brancusi's unique park in Tirgu Jiu as it was on his sculptural practices. Noguchi understood that Tirgu Jiu, in its overall conception, could be equated with the great Japanese Zen gardens. In Rikyū, Noguchi had sensed not only a remarkable nonconformist, but an adept of the total work of art. Noguchi's younger admirers, among them Teshigahara, were well prepared, by the 1980s, to reexamine Rikyū. Their preoccupation foreshadowed a serious reconsideration both of the avant-garde precepts they had entertained previously and the vexing issue of identity. As the contemporary critic Tarō Amano remarked, "the word 'identity' (although it was already in use in the 1970s) did not come into popular use among younger generation Japanese until sometime in the 1980s."[2]

Teshigahara's serious reassessment of the Muromachi and Momoyama periods was at least partly inspired by his rapprochement with Noguchi, whom he once called "the Rikyū of the modern period." Noguchi, who was constantly admonishing his friends to look to their own backyard, predicted that they would find that the Japanese have certain advantages; that sophisticated art forms such as Noh, tea ceremony, and garden design could offer a ground against which they would develop a distinctive modern art.

By the mid-1980s, Teshigahara began seeking a vehicle to express his thoughts adequately. This appeared in the form of a well-researched novel by Yaeko Nogami, *Hideyoshi and Sen no Rikyū*. The legendary Rikyū (many of the anecdotes about Rikyū must be regarded as legend) was vividly characterized in all his complexity. Teshigahara studied the Muromachi and Momoyama periods, prising out both the sumptuary aspects and the contrasting resistance epitomized by men of tea. During Rikyū's lifetime, a rich culture developed, with lavish castles and the building of public spaces demanding the services of artists and artisans. By contrast, there existed a strong current of Zen-inspired resistance epitomized by Rikyū's brilliant exploitation of the tea hut.

By pitching the conflict between Rikyū, the man of tea, whose genius was undeniable, and whose philosophy could shape a total environment, against the arriviste Hideyoshi, whose basic instinct was to be conspicuously lavish like the nouveau riche in any society, Teshigahara proposed a film in which the allegorical aspects were no longer suited to a surrealist-influenced vocabulary. Castles and tea huts became the settings for a political struggle, a duel, in which Teshigahara found many parallels with his own lifetime experience.

Suzuki's idealistic description of the spiritual meaning of the tea room as "the sense organ for a teaman to express himself"[3] is not left unchallenged. Suzuki believed that the conductor of the tea ceremony "makes everything vibrate with his subjectivity,"[4] but Teshigahara tried to depict the phenomenon in its broader aspect, one not unmixed with conflicting ideals.

The more obvious parallels with his own experience of political upheaval are not overemphasized, although Teshigahara chose a period in Japanese history in which huge social and political changes swept in as the old feudal domains were consolidated, and as forces from below, epitomized by the lowborn Hideyoshi, overcame the former rulers. The Japanese have a specific term for such a momentous historical shift, *gekokujō*: inferiors toppling superiors.

In the screenplay, on which Teshigahara collaborated with the painter, novelist, and former Dadaist, Genpei Akasegawa, Teshigahara took care to build the characters of the explosive and often crude Hideyoshi, and the reserved, superior genius Rikyū, with subtlety. He always allows for the unusual response of each of the protagonists so that they do not emerge as stereotypes. Rather, from Teshigahara's existentialist point of view, they are edged with the inevitable ambiguities implicit in universal human behavior.

He was careful to infuse his imagery with a spirit of authenticity. His detailed knowledge of calligraphy and traditional ceramic practices, as well as of the accoutrements in court life of the period, had been built up over the years. Like his friend Noguchi, Teshigahara had visited Kyoto's monasteries and engaged some of the more cultured monks in conversations. He knew the Zen temple settings that Rikyū himself had known. Teshigahara also established contact with the most important schools of tea ceremony and their *iemoto*, and when the time came, enlisted them as advisers.

For the character of Rikyū, he seems to have drawn inspiration from the well-known portrait attributed to Hasegawa Tōhaku (1539–1610) in which Rikyū is seen wearing the raiment of a lay Buddhist, his large and distinctive facial traits rendered as gravely thoughtful. This portrait was commissioned by one of the founders of Raku ware—the pottery in which Rikyū had revolutionized the art of making tea bowls by asking the potter Chōjirō (1516–92) to hand-model a rough, irregular bowl (a momentous event in the history of tea utensils that Teshigahara briefly remarks in the film). The portrait carries an inscription by Shun'oku Shūen, a priest at Daitokuji, and a friend and an instructor of

Portrait of Sen no Rikyū attributed to Hasegawa Tōhaku, ca. late 16th century. Ink and color on silk, 80.6 x 36.7 cm. Sen Sōsa Collection, Kyoto.

Tea bowl owned by Sen no Rikyū, called "Amadera," by Sasaki Chōjirō, ca. late 16th century. Raku ware, height 8.5 cm.

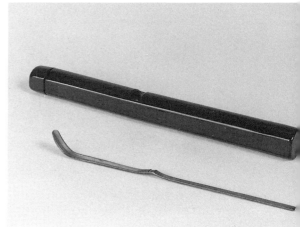

Tea scoop crafted by Sen no Rikyū, called "Namida" (tears), 1591. Bamboo, height 16.3 cm. Tokugawa Art Museum.

Flower container crafted by Sen no Rikyū.
Bamboo, height 33.4 cm. Tokyo National
Museum.

Rikyū, written just a few years after Rikyū's death. It reflects Teshigahara's perception of the master:

> Hat on his head and fan in his hand
> The solemn image he left behind captures what he always was.
> Like Zhao Zhou he sits awhile and drinks tea.
> This old man seems to gain knowledge without struggle.
>> Sokei showed me Layman Rikyū's portrait and asked
>> me to write an inscription, so I have written a four-
>> line verse and offer this with incense.
>> Fourteenth day, ninth month, fourth year of Bunroku
>> (1595) Sangen, Old Shun'oku Shūen.[5]

Hasegawa Tōhaku, a close associate of Rikyū, was a highly cultured
painter, whose comments on the history of painting were among the first
truly art historical writings in Japan. His texts indicate his familiarity with
the sages of the past, including Yoshida Kenkō, a forerunner of Rikyū in
the advocacy of simplicity: "Whatever the object, its perfection represents a fault. Leave things unfinished."[6] Kenkō's philosophy, "truly the
beauty in life is its uncertainty," penetrates Tōhaku's paintings, which

do not unfurl in time like the old scrolls but seize a temporary image. His landscapes depict a reality that is only intermittently perceived and suggests an instantaneous effect. Rikyū's aesthetic, reflected in the many anecdotes gathered a hundred years after his death and expressed in a few *waka* of his period, was shared by Tōhaku, who had possibly spent hours of discussion in Rikyū's teahouse.

For the film, Teshigahara engaged Rentarō Mikuni to play the role of Rikyū, admonishing him to avoid "surface acting." Mikuni immersed himself for several months in the study of the tea ceremony, and began to make many connections with his own profession of theater. The gravity of the portrait of the old man "who seems to gain knowledge without struggle" became Mikuni's model. Casting himself back, Mikuni set out to find an authentic "essence," as he says, and mentions particularly how Teshigahara used first a real tea bowl of the epoch and then a replica, and how he, Mikuni, could *feel* the difference. This, Mikuni believes, came through on the screen.

Teshigahara's attempt to establish an authentic human drama begins with the script he and Akasegawa wrote, but develops, as always with Teshigahara, in the working, with considerable attention to the thoughts of his collaborators, and whenever possible, improvisation. Kishida, who played the wife of Hideyoshi, stresses Teshigahara's unusual flexibility, and his willingness to take suggestions from his artists. In the scene in which Hideyoshi repairs to his home, complaining to his wife about the behavior of his retainers, it was Kishida who conceived of the excellent scene in which she clips his toenails and they converse intimately in Nagoya dialect.

Teshigahara's turn to the well-trod path of the Japanese costume drama surprised many of his contemporaries, who attributed it to his new role as *iemoto*. The long history of the period film in Japan is, however, intimately linked to political history. Film, during the prewar years, became a mask for views that were not tolerated by a censorious regime.

By the time Teshigahara took up the genre of period films, there was no further need to mask unorthodox views, but the political aspect remained. He felt a need to find contemporary meaning in political history. His approach had little in common with the conventional samurai drama.

In both traditional Japanese period films and Western films, such as those on Napoleon or the ancient Romans, the directors do not strive to

Scene from Rikyū; *Hideyoshi visiting his wife Nene.*

draw the viewer into a present. They create, rather, elaborate fantasies of a past. But Teshigahara's approach could never have been so remote since, to this day, there are men in monasteries in Japan dressed as in the seventeenth century, or, as in the shrine at Ise, dressed as the men in the earliest of picture scrolls. Students and intellectuals still seek out these men, consulting them on ancient philosophies and seeking the origins of their own thoughts, as did Noguchi, who constantly plied his friends in the monasteries with aesthetic questions. Because ancient art forms such as the Noh theater, Kabuki, and the tea ceremony still subsist in modern Japan, the historic drama can never be as remote as it is in the West. Teshigahara tried to bring Rikyū and Hideyoshi close, just as he tried as a youth to bring Hokusai to life by showing real hands working the wood blocks.

In the contrapuntal scenes of the film, Teshigahara frames selected environments in order to bring to life the events of the period. His concern for detail, which is always marked in his films, is not based on a pedantic will to be authentic, but rather, on his own perceptions as a working artist who had practiced almost all the skills required by Rikyū for the man of tea. He had intimate acquaintance with the gestures: while sitting at his work table at Echizen, swiftly fashioning a Raku style tea bowl; while cutting his own bamboo brushes or clay utensils; while creating haiku with a large brush; while participating in the tea ceremony offered at Urasenke; while attending the firing of the kiln and experimenting with rare glazes. The film would be, as the historian Seizō Hayashiya points out, a means for Teshigahara to understand himself as an avant-garde artist, which he would only achieve *after* having made the film.

With his conviction that "fundamental human problems do not change," Teshigahara undertook to find the key situations in the lives of the two men, Rikyū and Hideyoshi, dramatize them, and place them in history in such a way as to induce viewers to see parallels with contemporary events. He worked with key themes: the assimilation of foreign ideas and inventions by the warlords of the latter sixteenth century; the brutal cross-purposes always at work in political life; the presence of artistic currents that contravene reigning ideas of power; and the crisis of conscience always lurking in the psyche of the true artist. Rikyū's life, which is represented historically as a life of contemplation (although his entanglement with Hideyoshi suggests that his spirituality was not entirely unsullied) is contrasted with the life of the man of action: harassed, always threatened by court intrigues, and driven by forces beyond his understanding. Judging by the film, Teshigahara was not unmindful of the frequent distortions in accounts of Zen Buddhism, which dwell on the beauty and eloquence of the arts of Zen and play down the often ruthless behavior of Zen monks who freely participated in political life and were at times as bellicose and violent as the daimyo they opposed.

Rikyū's often silent presence at momentous events in the film leaves a trace of suspicion in the viewer's mind, as Teshigahara leads him to his first crisis of conscience when he is directed by Hideyoshi to poison a rival daimyō, Ieyasu, and Rikyū tacitly refuses. This crucial scene was filmed again and again, always in the presence of advisers from Urasenke who monitored each gesture. Teshigahara restrained the actors so that the scene has a slow, almost ritualistic character and focused on the importance of objects, as he had done so often in his previous films, most particularly the objet d'art containing the poison.

Teshigahara established the key mood in his very first scene which focuses on Rikyū's hands and the bamboo dipper with which he ladles the water for the tea ceremony. The dipper, still in use today, was, as Okakura points out, the one object which was always new, always clean, in a ceremony where the ideal of oldness (*wabi*) prevails. "The mellowness of age is over all, everything suggestive of recent acquirement being tabooed save only the one note of contrast furnished by the bamboo dipper and the linen napkin, both immaculately white and new."[7]

The opening scene, a slow re-enactment of an old anecdote passed down through history, emerges from the diffuse light of early dawn, with the subdued sounds of trickling water. The anecdote, as retold by Suzuki, concerns a day when Hideyoshi, having heard of Rikyū's magnificent garden of morning glories, expressed the wish to see them. When he arrived, there was not a single morning glory in the garden. When he entered the tea room, however, there, in isolated splendor, is a solitary morning glory.

Teshigahara builds slowly to the climactic moment. First, he shows Hideyoshi and his entourage hastening through the dim garden. This he does by filming the rapid pace of Hideyoshi's feet—almost trotting—as they negotiate the *roji* (the irregularly set path of stepping stones which usually symbolizes the approach, away from the world, into the microcosm of peaceful contemplation in the teahouse itself). This scene alone is a discreet hint of the inability of the man of power to leave the contentious world of his political life behind. As Hideyoshi crawls through the traditionally narrow, lowset doorway, he sees the single bloom and holds his tongue. The two men then commune through the stately rhythms of the tea ceremony as they prepare tea for each other.

Throughout the film, Teshigahara holds to the pace of the ritual, slow and subtle, whenever Rikyū is on camera, and quickens whenever Hideyoshi is performing. Historical events, such as the flashback in which Hideyoshi is still a vassal of Nobunaga, whose importation of muskets from Europe had guaranteed his victories in battle, inform the viewer of Japanese interest in European ideas. Teshigahara shows the reception of a Portuguese embassy and the demonstration of improved muskets, as Hideyoshi looks on. The line in this scene, "Land has no end," introduces the abruptly changing world view with which the players in Hideyoshi's time had to contend. Teshigahara further explores contemporary life in Hideyoshi's palace early in the film by showing the company of actors, led by Teshigahara's close friend, the Noh actor Hideo Kanze, who, as they prepare and eat their communal dinner, discuss the political situation and try to adapt, in self-interest, to the day's news. As Teshigahara stresses, the political climate will always impinge on their artistic life.

Three scenes from Rikyū *(1989). Rikyū and Hosokawa Tadaoki being served tea at Furuta Oribe's tea house.*

Hideyoshi gazing sternly at a globe of the world in a pivotal moment in the film.

Rikyū supervising a firing at Chōjirō's kiln.

Other juxtapositions occur, building up the conflict between artistic and political ends. Teshigahara shows the lavish headquarters of Hideyoshi and his treasury of gold, and mentions the gold tea room he had once demanded—and according to legend, received—from Rikyū. Immediately after, Teshigahara takes us to the kiln where Rikyū, with great concentration, supervises the firing of a vessel. We are shown the bowl first at record heat—a lambent scarlet, in close-up—and then as it cools, transformed by a rich black glaze. Rikyū's uncompromising nature is suggested when, despite Hideyoshi's expression of displeasure with black utensils, Rikyū persists. The first dark hint of the tragedies to come occurs when Hideyoshi orders Rikyū's student and friend at the kiln to be banished.

Throughout the film Teshigahara alternates scenes in which artists—painters, actors, *chajin*—perform their functions both at the palace and in the flourishing Kyoto monasteries, and scenes in which Rikyū appears as a kind of superior aesthetic presence whose sovereign calm is rarely disturbed until the fateful moment when he decides to oppose the tyrant's scheme to invade China. From that moment, Teshigahara accelerates the pace of events, showing a dramatic scene at the temple in which Rikyū's effigy is savagely attacked and sundered by furious soldiers, a stately march of the exiled tea master through a bamboo grove, a misty water scene as he and his wife depart forever from privilege and protection, and the denouement, with Rikyū brought down, preparing to comply with Hideyoshi's demand that he commit ritual suicide.

Teshigahara's accomplishment with this film, in which the period genre was enhanced, was widely remarked. The film won an award in the International Film Festival in Montreal for "the best artistic contribution" and was praised by the writer Peter Grilli in *The New York Times* for its compelling treatment, both as a historical epic and as the psychological interaction of two fascinating personalities. "With the confrontation of art and power as its central theme, and an era of social ferment and explosive cultural innovation as its setting, the parallels of *Rikyū* with present-day Japan are not hard to see,"[8] Grilli wrote, praising Teshigahara's grasp of the complexities of cultural politics in sixteenth-century Japan.

Encouraged by the generally warm reception, Teshigahara embarked on another period film, conceived as a sequel, this time documenting the rise and fall of one of Rikyū's friends, his contemporary and disciple, Furuta Oribe, whose rather different style is commemorated in ceramics called "Oribe ware." While far less coherent and marred by the doll-like star's mediocre performance in the role of Princess Goh, who is said to be resistant to authority, the film *Basara*, alternately titled, *The Princess Goh*, nonetheless contains some splendid reconstructions of the physical ambiance of the period and a few memorable moments of high drama, this time between Oribe and his patron, Ieyasu. There are also a few glimpses, anachronistically, of Teshigahara's own inventions in the art of installing bamboo structures. This film, which falls occasionally into the banal coinage of the Japanese period film, nonetheless advanced Teshigahara's own interest in the details of Japan's artistic and political history, and most particularly, in the way that foreign ideas and philosophies, as well as religions, were entwined with local events.

NOTES

1 Akiyama, *Japon des Avant Gardes*, p. 487.

2 Tarō Amano, "Some Issues of Circumstance: Focusing on the 1990s," in *Japanese Art after 1945: Scream Against the Sky*, Yokohama, 1994, p. 28.

3 Daisetz Suzuki, *Zen and Japanese Culture*, Tokyo, 1988, p. 306.

4 Ibid., p. 307.

5 *Japan, The Shaping of Daimyō Culture, 1185–1868*, National Gallery of Art, Washington, 1988, p. 88.

6 Linhartova, *Sur un Fond Blanc*, p. 190.

7 Kakuzō Okakura, *The Book of Tea*, trans. Everett F. Bleiler, New York, 1964, p. 36.

8 Peter Grilli, *The New York Times*, Sept. 24, 1989, p. H15.

11

*O*nce the psychological barrier to the past had been breached, Teshigahara, with his usual exuberance, sought to expand his province. From the late 1980s to the present, many of his activities, both as an impresario—a kind of latter-day Diaghilev—and as an artist, indicate his will to vault boundaries amongst the arts, not only boundaries traditionally separating them, but those separating the imaginative realm into past and present. While fulfilling his endless duties as *iemoto*, Teshigahara nonetheless found, or rather, created for himself many situations in which to expand upon his new sense of freedom.

From the outset of his professional life, Teshigahara had shown a strong proclivity for the arts that entailed collaboration. His exploration of the Japanese aesthetic past only served to reinforce his belief in the value of sharing artistic impulses with artistic colleagues. Nearly all of the arts he practiced had always required either the support or the active participation of others, ranging from flower arrangement, which demands the aid of skilled assistants, to filmmaking, to his large enterprises such as mass tea ceremonies in which he engaged the talents of other artists and architects. Most of his collaborators, ranging from his old comrades of the 1950s to a few much younger figures, such as the architect Tadao Andō, shared a keen interest in finding inspiration both in the past and the present, and in resurrecting viable Japanese traditions, including that of artistic collaboration.

A presence in the intellectual life of Teshigahara's circle is the poet Makoto Ōoka, for example, whose poems Teshigahara has rendered in calligraphy. Ōoka delved deeply into Japanese traditions, and around 1970, began to engage other poets in the practice of the unique Japanese form known as the *renga*, or the linked poem. His background as a young Surrealist supported this inquiry. André Breton and his poet friends had experimented with collaborative poems and had always held sacred the famous line by Lautréamont: "Poetry is made by all, not one." Ōoka had written in depth on one of the most luminous Surrealist poets, Paul Eluard, in 1952, and was steeped in Surrealist lore.

The move toward *renga* was natural enough. Twenty years after his first experiments, Ōoka wrote an essay on the meaning and contemporary possibilities in the practice of the *renga* form. In *The Colors of Poetry*, Ōoka notes:

> I have long been interested in the fact that in the Japanese arts, as well as such hobbies as flower arranging, the tea ceremony, and the like, one clear tendency or principle can be seen. It is the liking people have for calling together their comrades and forming "associations" (*kessha*), "coterie magazines" (*dōjin-zasshi*), and "arts groups" (*bijutsu dantai*) as well as the various schools of flower arranging, tea ceremony, and the like . . . Why is it the Japanese so much like to gather together?[1]

Ōoka explores the question by examining various poetic traditions, and most particularly, the elaborate traditions of *renga* which reveal "the continuing interplay, sometimes struggle, between the banquet (*utage*) of communal involvement and the private vision of the solitary mind (*koshin*)." In his summary, Ōoka talks about the exceptional value of the shared experience in linked free-verse writing which brought him close friendships with his fellow poets from other countries:

> This experience has made me rethink the essence, the very spirit of linked verse as it underlies Japanese poetic history. It is important to recognize that from earliest times, the classic Japanese verse structure of 5–7–5–7–7, along with its components 5–7–5 and 7–7, was respected, even venerated as "a gift of words" which worked as a catalyst to forge ties among people. So the classic formal poetry we have been considering is actually a refined form of interpersonal communication.[2]

Ōoka's observations parallel those of the great Mexican poet, Octavio Paz, who first visited Japan in 1952 and immediately engaged in the study of Japanese poetic traditions, later translating Bashō's haiku into Spanish. In 1969, Paz gathered three other poets from France, Britain, and Italy and undertook a five-day, intensive *renga* session in Paris. Paz had been deeply affected by his early concourse with Breton and had long been interested in the Surrealist notion of the collective poetic work. His experience with *renga* was recalled in his introduction to the book that resulted from the Paris session, published by Gallimard in 1971:

> I perceive two modes of affinity: the first, the element of combination which governs the renga, coincides with one of the central preoccupations of modern thought, from the concerns of logic to the experiments of artistic creation; the second, the collective character of a game, corresponds with the crisis of the notion of the author, and with the aspiration towards a collective poetry.[3]

Paz wrote that the Surrealists brought an end to the idea of an author by resolving the contradiction of the romantics: "The poet is merely the place of meeting, the field of battle and of reconciliation of the impersonal and masked forces that inhabit us." A serious student of Eastern philosophies, Paz points out that the practice of *renga* implies the negation of certain cardinal Western notions, such as the belief in the soul and the reality of the I, which he maintains was fought in its own way by Buddhism, Confucianism, and Shintoism:

> For all these reasons, it seems to me that the *renga* must have offered to the Japanese the possibility of going out from themselves, of passing from the anonymity of isolated individual into the circle of exchange and recognition. Also it was a way of liberating themselves from the weight of hierarchy. Although it was governed by rules as strict as those of etiquette, its object was not to put a brake on personal spontaneity but to open up a free space so that the genius of each one could manifest itself without doing harm either to others or oneself.[4]

Paz describes the session as a test, a "purgatory in miniature." Ōoka's testimony is similar. It is not easy for the modern poet, from Japan or Mexico or France or Italy, with the modern habits of solitude and individualism, to adapt himself to sharing the poetic impulse. But the value is great, both poets agree, for it brings a kind of mutual discovery and moves toward the resolution of the tension that always exists between individuals and the group on all levels. In addition, the survey of the *renga* tradition shores up the modern poet's conviction that he can, as did the great modernists Pound and Eliot, translate the experiences of colleagues in the past into the idiom of the present. Just reading the commentaries of Shinkei written in 1463 on the nature of linked verse could inspire the contemporary artist or poet. Shinkei, in his treatise, *Sasamegoto*, defined the art of *renga* as "not the art of composing poems, or verses of a poem, but a spiritual exercise to penetrate the talent and vision of another."[5] He also observed that "to follow one's own bent is not the way to experience the indecipherable meaning of others."[6]

From his youth, when he collaborated with Kōbō Abe, Teshigahara seems to have felt a deep need to discover the "indecipherable meaning of others." Many of his films probed the existential problem, already recognized by Shinkei, of the "meaning of the others," and many of his undertakings, such as his film on Gaudí, were clearly meant to "penetrate the talent and vision of another." He longed to participate in what Ōoka calls the "banquet," but he also knew the passion of the individual artist whose drive is to shape the musings of his "solitary mind."

With the experience of *Rikyū* fresh in his mind, Teshigahara began to imagine a kind of communal activity that would marshal the talents of his friends and resurrect the legendary mass tea ceremony staged by Hideyoshi in which Rikyū and other tea masters, including Hideyoshi himself, served hundreds of citizens. The great tea party of 1587 in Kyoto was meant to last for ten days, but for unknown reasons was called off after the first day.

Teshigahara's first experiment with the grand tea event occurred in 1992 when he utilized the garden at the Imperial Villa in Numazu, a seaside resort. Elated by the rich growth of ancient pine trees and the savor of the salt blowing in from the sea, Teshigahara envisioned a modern variation on the ancient tea ceremony.

Teshigahara engaged three major architects, all friends—Arata Isozaki, Tadao Andō, and Kiyonori Kikutake—to conceive of a modern teahouse, designed to receive guests for the ceremony. Teshigahara himself joined them, constructing a large oval bamboo structure and his characteristic tunnels of arching bamboo. Isozaki brought together his two traditions—modernism from France and Japanese architectural modes of building—in constructing what one journalist described as a square structure raised to second-floor level resembling a tree house. Isozaki pointedly titled it, "The Drunken Boat," reminding his viewers of his old love for the poetry of Arthur Rimbaud. Andō used *washi* paper and protected his round, accordion-pleated teahouse under a paper umbrella.

A writer in the *International Herald Tribune*, reviewing the month-long celebration, thought that, "Teshigahara shows his eye as a film director in his Numazu installation. The maze of wavelike domes and bamboo screens is a movie set of sorts: a dreamscape which palpitates with the breeze, masking its surroundings in a tangled web of shadows."[7]

Teshigahara was widely quoted in the press at the time, saying that he conceived of the tea ceremony as "performance art that borrows from every discipline." He stressed to interviewers that the original teahouse was never formal architecture, but rather a *sōan*, a temporary hermitage. The *chashitsu* should have, he said, "the character of an impromptu place." The whole performance at Numazu was, he said, in an "improvisational mood." Beyond the aesthetic character of the tea ceremony, Teshigahara discerned a social purpose similar to that of the *renga*. In the tea ceremony, he says, there arises a kind of friendship. "People of different occupations and social classes gather to share the singular opportunity in one meeting, with the space and time organized only through the tea ceremony."[8]

Emboldened by the success of the Numazu event, Teshigahara began planning an unprecedented extravaganza: a huge tea ceremony for the garden of the UNESCO building in Paris. Although Rikyū's concept of *wabi*—the taste for simplicity and quietude—could not survive the concentrated energies of the urban setting, Teshigahara had in mind to sequester the vast and polyglot populace of Paris in tiny structures conceived by artists and architects from Europe and Japan and enable them to participate in an art form that inevitably engages exchange. The spirit of theater, of play, of ensemble, of improvisation would, he hoped, break the barriers between East and West.

One of Teshigahara's collaborators for the event, the tea master Masakazu Izumi, summed it up when he wrote of the complexity of the

The Drunken Boat *teahouse by Arata Isozaki. Numazu, 1992.*

Paper teahouse by Tadao Andō. Numazu, 1992.

Daen teahouse by Teshigahara. Numazu, 1992.

tea ceremony with its interplay of so many art forms, but remarked that, "In fact, through this act which consists in drinking tea, it is the encounter with others that is important . . . As in an orchestra, each element that composes the ceremony must play its proper part, while respecting the harmony of the ensemble." Teshigahara, a practiced orchestrator and conductor, had to balance the implicit contradictions (the lavishness of the Parisian setting against the spirit of *wabi* and the individualism of the creators of the tea huts against the communal aspects of the open-air tea ceremony).

In the classic periods of Japanese history, there were clear distinctions between *hare*, the public aspect of life, and *ke*, the private. Here in the heterogeneous setting of Paris, the distinctions could not be clearly established since the visitors to a modern tea hut had to be hustled in and out rather quickly in order to accommodate their numbers, and the privacy established by the architects was at best a glimpse of thought.

Still, in his quest for a universal principle, some level at which all human beings can meet, Teshigahara conceived of this immensely complicated project as a "dialogue of cultures" and as a means to unite East and West on the common ground of the sole art form, which according to him, included the spectator as artistic participator. In his statement for the press, Teshigahara stressed that the tea ceremony itself was "an expression, evolved through the influence of various products of civilization which were introduced from China, Korea, Southeast Asia, and from faraway Europe." The composite art form, he said, was an avant-garde art that integrated objects, environment, and time into an aesthetic unity. The collaborators he invited—architects, artists, and designers Tadao Andō, Jai Eun Choi, Charlotte Parriand, Ettore Sottsass, and the tea master Masakazu Izumi—reflected the wide range of nationality and age that Teshigahara foresaw as both an opening to avant-garde thoughts and an endorsement of a usable tradition.

Teshigahara himself, by laying out with great artifice a bamboo setting, bound it together. He created the *roji*, a long bamboo tunnel with its flickering light and shadow through which visitors would enter the UNESCO gardens, and several propitious bamboo installations guiding the steps of the guest artists. One of the participants, the 90-year old designer Charlotte Parriand, once an associate of Le Corbusier, spoke with great reverence of Teshigahara's conception, pointing out that the musicality of the ensemble of bamboo structures reminded her of the undulating wall of La Tourette that Le Corbusier had rendered in human scale.

As the conductor of this orchestral, or theatrical, event, Teshigahara played out his old dream of bringing together unlike things and people and creating something new. His own bamboo compositions served as both link and segment, much as in *renga*. The effect of his own ephemeral art of installation, using the temporary material of bamboo exclusively, bore out his view that, "My art has a pact with time."

The enormous effort for the UNESCO event lasted only fifteen days, but those days remained memorable for many witnesses and participants. The veteran art critic Pierre Restany later wrote of Teshigahara's "covered alleys, swept paths, tunnels, closed spaces, roofs in vegetal arcades" as having a rigorous logic produced by the maximum utilization of the physical properties of bamboo. "While we are in the heart of this trembling and sensuous vegetal space," he wrote, "the impression that seizes us is that of a fugitive beauty and a totally provisional harmony." Such structures, he said, are not made to last, but rather "to inscribe themselves in the visual memory with a paroxistic shock or retinal persistence."[9]

The elaborate garden project was not Teshigahara's only contribution to the Parisian festival of Japanese art. Once again he collaborated with his old friend Hideo Kanze, whose lineage descends from ancient Noh masters, but who had experimented widely with Western theater in his youth, having directed plays for the Abbey Theatre and for the Berliner Ensemble before he returned to the Noh theater at the age of fifty-two. Kanze took the chief role in the Paris performance of "The Woman and Her Shadow," a Noh-style play written in 1923 by Paul Claudel, then the French ambassador to Japan. For the Parisian production, Teshigahara replaced the traditional *hashigakari* (the bridge that in conventional Noh plays connects the dressing room of the actors with the stage, and that symbolized the passage from one world to another) with a tunnel of bamboo arches. The stage set he designed used vertical bamboo poles, some with palm-like crests, as spatial organizers of the Western-style stage.

As the stately rhythms of the traditional Noh play unfold, the bamboo is magically transformed, now casting pulsating shadows against a back screen, now darkly portentous in their vertical rigor. Kanze saw the central bamboo pole as a symbolic dividing line between the living and the dead, and Teshigahara, he felt, seized the spirit of the modern rendition of Claudel's play by suggesting the two psychological realms implicit in Claudel's script. Kanze performed his role in the traditional Noh style, but altered it slightly, almost imperceptibly, to merge ancient and modern. "If you have in mind to preserve a tradition, it is not worth preserving," he says.

In Teshigahara's next grand project incorporating bamboo, his ambition was rather different. Invited to make an installation at the Contemporary Art Museum designed by Tadao Andō on Naoshima Island, Teshigahara paced the spaces surrounding the resort-hotel museum, taking into consideration both the natural beauty of its seaside setting and the austere design of Andō's museum. In some ways, it is the eye of the filmmaker at work.

As the ferry from Takamatsu glides into port, Teshigahara's embellished slope leading up to Andō's concrete building is immediately perceived—a work of art at ground level. Teshigahara introduces the visitor to a unique spatial experience. He has followed the contours of the slope adjoining a splendid granite stairway designed by Andō and created a giant *tatami* with thousands of split bamboo elements forming a kind of carpet; or perhaps, rather than a carpet, some wondrous garment, with gentle folds, protecting the ground. This horizontality, endemic to the Japanese tradition of spaces perceived at floor level, provides a remarkable contrast to Andō's severe design.

From this wide-lens, panning entry, Teshigahara moves into a vertical rhythm, embracing the building with thickets of bamboo structures and leading the visitor indoors to the pièce de résistance: a huge, quasi-circular exhibition hall which he has converted into a phantasmagoric impression of cascading, sloping, tunneling, opening, many-leveled spaces. Green bamboo turned inside-out creates an almost aquatic interior atmosphere, while long elements, their notched interiors revealed, establishing a rhythm throughout, unite the lofty spaces created by Andō, transforming them into a sensuous experience not of walls and edges, but of a coursing interior of visual and kinetic adventure, remote from familiar rectilinear room spaces. A totally different experience. It is a true environmental circumlocution of the spectator that incites his participation. He moves with Teshigahara from frame to frame, as in a film, while the minute time segments accumulate into a whole.

The back terraces of the museum, with a sweeping view of the sea,

Teshigahara's bamboo installation at the Contemporary Art Museum designed by Tadao Andō, Naoshima Island, September-October, 1993.

were adorned by Teshigahara with bamboo structures not unlike the elliptical outdoor tea ceremony structure in Paris, forming a continuum with the previous bamboo experiences, and more or less converting the entire museum into an ambiguous center of a natural exterior.

Teshigahara's ambition to incite in the viewer a sense of contrast between nature and culture, concrete and bamboo, resort hotel and museum, physical heights and depths, tradition and innovation, was realized in Naoshima on a scale he had not yet previously approached. The ideal of the total work of art implicit in his entire artistic life came close to fulfillment.

But perhaps it was in another vast adventure of 1992 that the old operatic concept was fully activated in the great tradition established by Wagner with his idea of *Gesamtkunstwerk*. Naturally enough, this new avenue of expression for Teshigahara came in the form of an invitation to direct an opera in Europe.

Kent Nagano, a man who, while much younger, shares many of Teshigahara's basic convictions, had the inspired idea to invite Teshigahara to design and oversee a new production of the opera *Turandot* in Lyons. Nagano, whose Japanese grandparents had emigrated to California, sees himself as a man of the West. Although "one can still sense one's roots," he says, he stresses in interviews that "the world is interesting everywhere."[10] Appointed musical director of the National Orchestra of Lyons in 1989, Nagano quickly organized a program that would demonstrate his breadth of interests and his international stance.

His discovery of Teshigahara, that struck him initially like a thunderbolt, as he has said, came through a friend, the composer George Benjamin. When Benjamin saw *Woman in the Dunes* on British television, and shortly after on screen, he telephoned Nagano and urged him to see the film. He was certain that Nagano would see that Teshigahara's style would suit the operatic stage. Nagano had been thinking about *Turandot* and, after seeing the film, immediately got in touch with Teshigahara with his proposal.

Nagano's own interest in *Turandot*, the last and unfinished opera of Giacomo Puccini before his death in 1924, stemmed precisely from the fact that Puccini hadn't had the time to make revisions or write new versions. *Turandot*, he says, is not as smooth as *Tosca* or *Madame Butterfly*. It is more raw, powerful. "Puccini tried something new. The harmonic language of this opera is very twentieth century."[11]

The opera, much admired by Stravinsky and other twentieth-century composers, was conceived by Puccini after seeing an extravagant production of the eighteenth-century play by Carlo Gozzi staged by the German experimental director Max Reinhardt. Puccini set to work gathering historical references, listening to Chinese music on an old music box, and haunting museums. He asked his librettists to prepare something "that would make people weep." He worked slowly, undermined by the onset of throat cancer that felled him in 1924. On his bed at his death was the sketch for the finale of the opera. Two years later, Arturo Toscanini mounted the first performance of *Turandot* at La Scala in Milan. On the first evening, he lay down his baton, turned to the audience and said: "Here the opera by the maestro finishes." For the second performance, he included the finale, structured respectfully by Franco Alfano from Puccini's notes.

Gozzi's drama provided an ideal opportunity for Puccini to depart from the veristic approach of his previous operas. The play is couched in the terms of a fable. The Princess, Turandot, who, as Puccini said, "had brooded for so long under the ashes of her pride," is a cold and pitiless figure who poses three riddles to each suitor. If they fail to answer correctly, they are swiftly beheaded. When Calaf appears and answers correctly, he is the key that unlocks her heart, and she is transformed, as in many a fairy tale. But Puccini's librettists, when he asked for "a fairy tale, a fantastic subject, human and moving, beyond the beaten path," had fashioned a complicated drama in which the slave girl, Liu, who is in love with Calaf, sacrifices herself to save him. The range of intrigue and smoldering emotion is wide in the retelling of Gozzi's fable and leaves ample space for interpretation.

From the moment he heard Nagano's proposal, Teshigahara immersed himself in the study of opera. He watched videos of various performances and listened repeatedly to records. Like many other opera goers, he found the traditional performances distressing. Usually the sets were feeble evocations of the European's exotic notion of Chinese pavilions and palaces, and the costumes more like comic opera parodies of ancient Chinese apparel. Performances often tended to imitate the style of Puccini's most successful previous operas, such as *La Bohème*. Teshigahara understood that the fabulous required the use of symbolism, and that the opera must be designed in a nonrealistic, almost abstract style.

When Teshigahara began assembling his team, he thought immediately of his old comrade Hideo Kanze. Kanze, with his rich history of experimental theater, including avant-garde nontraditional groups, could use his expertise in hieratical Noh theater to new ends. He was a prominent founder of *Seigei*, the Youth Art Theater, that, after the turbulent demonstrations of 1960, began to explore alternatives to the social-realist tradition of political commentary, turning to the more stylized techniques of Bertolt Brecht, and casting an eye toward contemporary French theatrical developments. Kanze's broad understanding of many theatrical traditions including those of the West made him an ideal partner in Teshigahara's transformation of *Turandot*.

Teshigahara instinctively sought to make *Turandot* into symbolic theater, much as his brilliant ancestors Zeami and Chikamatsu had transformed theater in their time. Every student of theater in Japan was thoroughly familiar with the aesthetics of these extraordinary theatrical thinkers, and Kanze, from a great family tradition, had imbibed their principles from childhood. The writings of Zeami (1363–1443), while indebted to Zen Buddhism, can be understood on a basic level as a universal doctrine of symbolism and have much in common with: the thoughts of Aristotle (mimesis is not imitation, but the imitation of an action, which at the furthest reaches can be an action of the imagination); Kleist, in his famous essay on marionettes; and Mallarmé, in his discussions of theater and dance. Zeami's idea of "linking all the artistic powers with one mind" parallels Kleist's arguments. He noted that marionettes appear to move, but it is not they but the strings that perform. "When these strings are broken, the marionettes fall."[12] In Noh theater, "What holds the parts together is the mind . . . The mind must be made the strings which hold together all the powers of the arts."[13] The parallel with Aristotle can be found in Zeami's discussion of the essence of performance:

> If the essence is a flower, the performance is its fragrance . . .
> It has been said, "What one should desire to imitate is skillfulness; what one should not imitate is skillfulness." To imitate is performance, to have achieved resemblance is essence.[14]

Even more available to the modern sensibility are the thoughts of Chikamatsu Monzaemon (1653–1725), the brilliant playwright of the unique Japanese puppet theater and Kabuki. Chikamatsu was himself combating a new tendency in Japanese theater to seek realistic conformism. Audiences in his day attended Kabuki where they expected the actors to resemble real figures in their practical lives. But this, Chikamatsu declared, does not take into account the real methods of art. "Art is something which lies in the slender margin between the real and the unrea. . . . It is unreal, and yet it is not unreal; it is real, and yet it is not real. Entertainment lies between the two."[15] He advocated stylization as the essential artistic means, and like Zeami, stressed the implications rather than the direct expression of various emotional states.

Teshigahara's decision to stylize *Turandot* on broadly abstract lines called upon the talents of Kanze, who choreographed the production with the stately precision of the Noh theater, distancing the characters from the pathos of conventional Italian opera. To enhance the effect of a fable rather than a realistic love story, Teshigahara encouraged the costume designer Tomio Mōri to produce extravagantly flowing costumes that in themselves served as symbols. Mōri used metallic fabrics, diaphanous veils, sail-like sleeves that at times seemed batlike, and hieratic colors to distinguish the crowd from the chief protagonists. George Benjamin recalled that, "the costumes were formed into bizarre angular shapes spreading from all sides behind and around the characters; enormously elongated arms projected menacing claws at their ends."[16] With these highly sculptural accessories, Kanze could develop the grand symbolic gestures basic to Noh performance where costumes always abet action.

Attentive to every detail, Teshigahara enlisted the talents of the makeup artist Reiko Kruk whose specialty, as she says, is "metamorphosis." Kruk studied the characters and tried, as she says, to give each personage a double—one that "goes further than a real person, but respects his own face and character." Teshigahara, whom Kruk admires as a "poet who writes with many different materials," discussed his conception with Kruk, but then gave her a free hand.

Teshigahara's special contribution was to transform the theater with some 4,000 bamboos, bringing them into the space beyond the stage and up to the second balcony. For the stage proper, he created four semi-opaque tunnels of arching bamboo on each side, from which the performers issued like butterflies from a cocoon. The bamboo created a universe appropriate to a fable and fused all the elements. The lighting

Teshigahara's stage set for the final scene in the opera Turandot, *Lyons, 1992.*

held to the stylizing pattern of Teshigahara's original conception, and as Benjamin said, together with the sculptural manipulation of the massed chorus, "contributed to the overall impression of a novel approach to music theater, starkly beautiful and above all, profoundly original."[17] An extra touch was provided by the huge calligraphies Teshigahara produced, announcing the princess's riddle in Japanese.

His fusion of Japanese tradition with a markedly European libretto and music was not lightly undertaken. Teshigahara had thought carefully about the implications, and had even, with his habitual forthrightness, sought out the possibilities of a contemporary symbolism. He and Kanze discussed the implications of the cruelty pervading the fable.

Teshigahara maintains that *Turandot* displays a brutal force but also a certain purity, having known the domination of an invader. Liu, on the other hand, represents pure, disinterested love—the hidden face of *Turandot*. The drama, Teshigahara insists, is contemporary, since human sentiment has never changed.

In his interview with *Liberation*, Teshigahara stated that, "Cruelty remains present on the planet, and is not only in the fables of the eighteenth century revised by musicians at the beginning of the twentieth. Often we try not to notice it, we turn away, but it exists in spite of us."[18] Kanze added, "What is 'useful' about cruelty is that if we really know it, we can combat it. In *Turandot*, the princess takes as a pretext the evil that has been inflicted in order to gratify a kind of ancestral hatred, without 'justification.' Puccini reveals the process of *vendetta* which is still current. Hate in the name of ancestors is mute, it projects all its energy in brutal acts. I think one must ask oneself: what love would obstruct all that?"

Both artists saw in their collaboration a means to express their resistance to hatred and vengeance, which they pointed out had not abated in current world affairs. Teshigahara's skill in forging artistic alliances, finding artists whose abilities and sentiments converge with his own, brought him to a fulfillment of the old ideal of the total work of art, not only in the beholding, but in the essence, as suggested by Zeami in his century and Wagner in his.

After *Turandot*, and Claudel's Noh play, it remained only for Teshigahara and Kanze to return to the prototype—traditional Noh—to confront the ideal of "essence." In the summer of 1994, Teshigahara participated in the Avignon Theater Festival, directing two traditional Noh plays and one contemporary Noh play, *Susanoo*, which Teshigahara dubbed a "Nohpera." With his usual bravado, Teshigahara undertook his experiment with the modernist's question: What would happen if? In tampering with the fixed tradition of Noh, Teshigahara intended to release new possibilities, to move outside the centuries-old framework in order to bring into high relief the essential and durable virtues of Noh drama. He found excitement in what he called the "mismatching" of elements,

Abandoned quarry setting for Susanoo *in Carrièrre de Boulbon near Avignon.*

and like a laboratory researcher, was constantly alert to what might happen as he mixed the expected with the unexpected.

His enterprise was greatly inspired by the unusual setting he chose in Avignon, the Carrièrre de Boulbon, an abandoned quarry of ocher stone towering above a space that formed an almost natural amphitheater. The quarry, hidden in the countryside fifteen kilometers from Avignon, requires a long approach on an unpaved road, which serves almost like the bridge in traditional Noh, separating the theatergoers from the bustle of Avignon and slowly drawing them into the magical realm of the quarry. Teshigahara, who had already in mind the decor of this spectacular setting, was immediately inspired by the possibility of an encounter between the mass of stone and a forest of bamboo. The juxtaposition of mineral and vegetable seemed to him a perfect analogue to the juxtaposition of worlds in the Noh—the world of the dead and that of the living.

The young poet Takayuki Kawabata wrote the libretto based on the ancient Japanese origin myth in which the founders of the Japanese archipelago, Izanagi and Izanami, create the god Susanoo. Izanami, in subsequently giving birth to the sun goddess, dies of her burns and descends to the realm of death. Susanoo, the inconsolable son, weep so mightily that he causes a deluge and outrages the gods. His mother returns to rescue him from his vast grief by devouring him and bringing him back to the realm of the dead, but is deflected by a "god of venerable age" who gives Susanoo a magical peach to ward off death.

Teshigahara's choice of a myth in which the principal character is a rebel once again mirrors his own rebellious instincts. He belongs to a long tradition of anti-tradition that in Japan has put forth many singular artists. Despite the common view that conformism is the cornerstone of Japanese culture, the Japanese language, with its many subtle distinctions, is replete with words that convey the idea of rebellion, eccentricity, and nonconformism: *kijin*, a person who is peculiar, strange; *kikyo*, something strange and unpredictable; *koseiteki*, a strong personality; *jirisuteki*, rationality unbounded by outside pressure and influence; *hangyakusha*, a rebel; *hantaisha*, dissenter; and *itan*, a heretic or heathen.[19]

For his team, Teshigahara turned to: Kanze, who played the "god of venerable age"; Kanze's colleague and friend, Masakuni Asami, who played Izanami; and a rising young Kyōgen actor, Mansai Nomura, who played Susanoo. The music was by Maki Ishii, an avant-garde composer, and the makeup was designed by Reiko Kruk.

Essential to Teshigahara's vision was the use of expressive costumes that could evoke the sculptural qualities in traditional Noh costumes. Tomio Mōri once again invented great flowing robes that not only enclosed the actors, setting them off from their bamboo environment, but also responded to the immensely subtle movements of the Noh actors, initiating an action that is completed in virtual space. These distinctive costumes were eminently plastic. When Susanoo collapses in a grief-stricken mound, he is like a stone. When he slowly dances to his operatic lament, the costume flows outward, like a sail, filling the space of the rectangular stage and linking visually, in its curving contours, with the bamboo-arched tunnels through which the protagonists appear.

The Noh actor Hideo Kanze performing in Susanoo.

The actor Mansai No-mura dancing in Su-sanoo.

Nomura, a remarkable actor, was able to use his costume in the absolutely traditional way, while yet infusing his role with an individuality that the audience could easily perceive. His performance was a perfect fusion of old and new, especially in a soliloquy when he spoke haltingly, and at a certain moment, used the superb Noh tactic of "no action," described by Zeami:

> Dancing and singing, movements and different types of miming are all acts performed by the body. Moments of "no action" occur in between. When we examine why such moments without actions are enjoyable, we find that it is due to the underlying spiritual strength of actors which unremittingly holds the attention.[20]

The stage action of the three actors is enhanced by the abstract design of bamboo tunnels and lofty lighting towers that Teshigahara dressed with plaited bamboo. Here, Teshigahara departs from tradition by abandoning the asymmetry and the symbolic pine tree on a painted backdrop in favor of a bamboo wilderness for the traditional residence of spirits. Bamboo, in Teshigahara's view, is a perfect foil for the dramatic action of the myth because of its unclassifiable status, neither plant nor tree, and its ephemeral opposition to the eternal rock of the quarry. With the shaped bamboo elements, Teshigahara created a convincing analogy to the time-before-time of the mythic events he recounts. As Tatsumi Shinoda remarked, it was more than a stage design—it was a theatrical environment:

> Instead of making the stage design confront the power of the cliff, Teshigahara spread shreds of bamboo all around the stage on the ground like the surface of a swelling ocean. This made the square stage appear as if it was floating . . . Because of the arrangement, the overwhelming influence of the cliff was absorbed and circulated around the floating stage . . .[21]

Teshigahara bridged the cultural gap between Japanese and European audiences by introducing a narrator, the Franco-Italian actress Anna Galiena, who appears during the first moments of his "Nohpera." Written into the script as "The Woman of Avignon," she is surrounded

Bamboo stage lighting towers for Susanoo, Avignon Theater Festival, 1994.

by children from Avignon who, with their elfin costumes, formed a sur-
rogate Noh chorus that was somewhat incongruous. Their coy movements distracted from the gravity of the narrative and seemed an
unnecessary concession to Western tastes, undermining Teshigahara's

attempt to reduce a contemporary performance to the essence characteristic of the Noh theater. All the same, *Susanoo*, thanks largely to the performance of the outstanding Noh actors and Teshigahara's audacious set, did create a precedent and confirmed what another invited performer to the Avignon festival, the venerable Kazuo Ōno, always maintained—that the future is found in the past and the past in the future.[22]

NOTES

1   Makoto Ōoka, *The Colors of Poetry*, trans. Takako and Thomas Lento, Michigan, 1991, p. 3.

2   Ibid., p. 133.

3   Jacques Roubaud, Edoardo Sanguinetti, and Charles Tomlinson, *Renga. A Chain of Poems*, London, 1979, p. 21.

4   Ibid., p. 24.

5   Ibid., p. 36.

6   Ibid., p. 36.

7   Carol Lufty, *The International Herald Tribune*, Oct. 23, 1992.

8   Interview, *Daily Asahi*, Nov. 2, 1992.

9   Pierre Restany, Sōgetsu archive typescript.

10   Kent Nagano, quoted in "Le Chef Nagano Mijote 'Turandot'," *Toute France*, April 1992.

11   Nagano, *Toute France*.

12   Zeami, *Sources of Japanese Tradition*, p. 291.

13   Zeami, ibid p. 291.

14   Zeami, ibid p. 291.

15   Chikamatsu Monzaemon, *Sources of Japanese Tradition*, p. 439.

16   George Benjamin, Sōgetsu archive typescript.

17   Benjamin, Sōgetsu archive.

18   Hideo Kanze and Hiroshi Teshigahara, interviewed by Dominique Dubreuil in *Lyons Liberation*, May 7, 1992.

19   I thank the painter, Paolo Suzuki, for this information.

20   Zeami, *Sources of Japanese Tradition*, p. 302.

21   Tatsumi Shinoda, *Asahi Evening News*, August 21, 1994.

22   *Alternatives Théâtrales*, p. 93.

12

*T*eshigahara and his generation faced innumerable problems that were in large measure circumstantial: the humiliation of the war, the destruction of the institutions within which they had been raised, the physical devastation of the places they had known as children. Above all, there was the egregious and unassimilable fact of Hiroshima and Nagasaki. As Ōoka forcefully put it:

> I was decisively affected by what happened on August 15, 1945; all values inculcated into my head during the war were overturned in a single day. We had been taught that Japan was right; it turned out to be wrong. The emperor had been a living god; he no longer was. And so forth. In the sphere of ideas, such as the existence or nonexistence of God, absolutism may have a place; it does not in our daily life. I take it for granted that there are many answers to one question, and that one question provokes many answers.[1]

Ōoka, who in the same interview stressed that he regarded himself as an extreme relativist with "strong doubts about anyone who takes any absolutist position," articulates the general attitudes of Teshigahara's circle of artistic colleagues. Almost all of Teshigahara's collaborators on his various projects are chary of absolutist stands, and at one time or another expressed their resistance to fixed attitudes, either about Japan or the world at large, or their aesthetic views.

There was nothing static in the period in which Teshigahara evolved as an artist. Unsettling events occurred regularly and demanded responses more insistently than they would in nations that had not known Hiroshima. Although the formation of an artist can never be measured or described in the crude formula of cause and effect, for Teshigahara and the major artists of his generation, many choices had to be made that related to public, historical circumstance.

The issues that had long preoccupied Japanese intellectuals—issues of identity, Westernization, local traditions, Eastern aesthetics—returned after the war with burning urgency. Philosophically, the role of contingency had to be confronted: how much had historical circumstance framed the national life; how much were these circumstances the product of some Hegelian logic; how much was the result of historical accident? Was there such a thing as a national character or had it been cleverly cobbled by Meiji propagandists? Was there something peculiar to Japanese arts and letters, or was this also a delusion sponsored by a hundred years of authoritarian tampering?

Since Teshigahara's generation was charged with building a totally new social and political structure, beginning, as they often said, from degree zero, it was almost impossible for the artists to turn away, to expunge their many doubts, and to spring free from mitigating circumstances. Teshigahara was no exception. His shifting interests brought him face to face with many of the shared problems, not the least of them the problem of his Japanese identity which he and most of his friends at first sought to evade and later (rejoining a rather long tradition) sought to confront. Teshigahara, while never indulging in polemics and rarely discussing his personal philosophical struggles, obviously gave considerable thought to the accident of fate that had given birth to him in a place called Japan. His attitudes were repeatedly challenged throughout his youth by the confusion that reigned in postwar Japan and the mere fact of being Japanese.

Unlike Mishima, who so often wrote with fine scorn of Westernizing elders who wore ridiculous English tweeds and bowler hats, or Tanizaki, who plaintively described the awkward adaptation of Western mores on the part of the Japanese bourgeoisie, Teshigahara and his friends were loath to condemn "progressive" members of the older intelligentsia. Teshigahara's attitude was straightforward, even in his youth. Some Japanese customs, affectionately recalled from his childhood, were good, even better than Western customs. Anyone can see, for instance, that a *yukata* is an extremely comfortable, practical mode of dress, especially in summer, so why not avail oneself of it? While Mishima's mission had much in common with that of nineteenth-century authors in Russia who passionately took sides in the argument between Slavophiles and Westernizers (an argument that is, alas, still nefariously at work in contemporary Russia), most of the other intellectuals in postwar Japan emphatically rejected the symmetrical arguments of the past and struggled toward a syncretic compromise in which the best features of Japanese culture would be honored but never enshrined in nationalist absolutism. Theirs was, and still is, a dynamic approach that, as Ōoka says, posits many answers to a single question and many questions to a single answer.

The dynamics of Teshigahara's development as an artist, the pattern of his choices, the alacrity with which he always responded to contingencies, often brought him into undertakings in which he could draw upon the traditions that everyone in his circle had at one time or another reconsidered. For instance, when Teshigahara decided to allegorize the story of Rikyū, he not only drew upon his own heritage as son of an *iemoto*, well grounded in Chinese classics and the specialized history of Zen approaches to ikebana, but also, as a serious film artist. In the course of developing his visual score, Teshigahara foraged in Kyoto where he studiously approached priests of famed monasteries and carefully examined the specific sites of famed gardens, above all that of Daitokuji.

The practical act of exploring a past for the purpose of refreshing the present is characteristic of Teshigahara's current approach. For whatever task he sets himself, he excavates the sources he needs, and often they lie within the culture in which he was formed. Since Japan's cultural history is far from monolithic, although it is so often misrepresented as composed of fixed patterns of thought, it is always possible for Teshigahara and his companions to find a consoling precedent. Teshigahara's long sustained interest in what is "universal" in human life—his basic leitmotif, in fact—finds many sources in various epochs of Japanese history. The neo-Confucianists, for instance, were quite eager to establish universality when they wanted to stimulate world trade. Fujiwara Seika (1561–1619) wrote to the Prince of Annam:

It will be seen therefore that men differ only in secondary details, such as clothing and speech. Countries may be a thousand or even ten thousand miles apart and difference may be found in clothing and speech but there is one thing in all countries which is not far apart, not a bit different, that is "good faith."[2]

Teshigahara's friends, and he himself, were careful to avoid identifying the great accomplishments in Japan's cultural past exclusively with nationality. When they considered certain indisputably Japanese aesthetic principles or traditions, they nearly always observed that there were counterparts in the West, or at least similar institutions. A concept such as that of *Yūgen* was usually examined both from the point of view of its historical presence in Japanese life over a period of centuries and from the point of view of its meaning for modern artists, not particularly modern *Japanese* artists. Unquestionably, when Teshigahara chose to create a *Turandot* that was entirely moored in Symbolism (a movement that spiraled through modern aesthetic history, liberally drawing upon ideas from both East and West), he could have found the grounds for his attitude in the concept of *Yūgen*, particularly as discussed by Nossé Asaji in a text every Japanese intellectual knew.

Originally, Nossé explains, the word *Yūgen* was used by Chinese philosophers to indicate something "profound and unfathomable, therefore not easily penetrated by the human mind," but as it entered medieval Japanese aesthetics, it took on the connotation of artistic excellence:

> This word indicates the endlessly expanding beauty of suggestiveness, the beauty of profundity that goes ever deeper.

In a footnote to his *Zen and Japanese Culture*, Daisetz Suzuki remarks:

> *Yūgen* is a compound word, each part, *yū* and *gen* meaning "cloudy impenetrability" and the combination meaning "obscurity," "unknowability," "mystery," "beyond intellectual calculability" but not "utter darkness."[3]

What Nossé calls the "endlessly expanding beauty of suggestiveness" was also the grounds for the French poetic movement initiated by

Mallarmé and studied intensely by twentieth-century Japanese poets and artists just after the war. If they thought about *Yūgen*, it was most often in comparative terms. Even their exploration of Zen Buddhism in general was often conducted in such a way as to tease out the principles that could be found in all artistic cultures. They were well aware of what Kitarō Nishida called the "historical actuality" of most theories, and believed with him that "only through comparison with other things can we achieve a true understanding of a given thing."[4] Nishida wrote:

> Needless to say, men as members of the same species, *homo sapiens*, have thought the same things often enough. However, even doctrines of a purely theoretical character are not independent of their historical backgrounds; discussion of them must therefore start with their historical bases and treat them as living things . . . [5]

The contemporary Japanese philosopher, Hide Ishiguro, has discussed Nishida's contribution to twentieth-century philosophy, stressing that his early book, *Enquiries into the Good*, was the work of "someone who participated in European philosophy even as he had deliberately educated himself in the traditional discipline of Zen." Nishida's system, she writes, tries to base our comprehension of reality, the good, and religion, on what he calls "pure experience." Certain commentators say that this notion of the pure experience comes from Buddhism, but in reality, Ishiguro maintains, it derives from William James, who advanced his "neutral monism" in the same epoch:

> One notices that there was a Zeitgeist, a point of view which inspired intellectuals everywhere, bypassing national frontiers and cultures. People were seduced by the notion of *données immédiates* or experiences presumed to be anterior to the distinction between subject and object. Not only William James, the American philosopher and psychologist, of whom Nishida speaks in this work, but Bergson and Husserl (two authors whom Nishida read with enthusiasm) and also Russell, constructed philosophical systems based on certain *données* that are experienced directly.[6]

Ishiguro adds that during the same period, the writer Sōseki Natsume wrote in the margin for the English translation (1910) of Bergson's *Essais sur les Données Immédiates de la Conscience*:

> It is not unusual to be touched by the beauty of an interesting literary work, but that almost never occurs apropos of a work of philosophy or science. This work is an exception. When I read what he had written on time and space in Section 2, I was struck by its beauty.[7]

Finally, what Ishiguro says about a philosophic tradition can as well be said about an aesthetic tradition and reflects the fundamental views advanced by Teshigahara and his artistic companions:

> A philosophic tradition is not a natural manifestation of the mentality of a people. Accidental encounters, deliberate choices, and even the decision to abandon things that one might have maintained, contribute also to forming a tradition. The philosophy that flourishes in Europe today has assimilated elements of foreign origin that are extremely varied: for example, during the Middle Ages, Aristotelian philosophy as conceived by the Arabs; in the nineteenth century, Indian philosophy as interpreted by the German idealists, and naturally, the ideas that come from Judaism, whether Talmudic or mystic . . . [8]

The dynamic vision of tradition always forming and never frozen is most congenial to Teshigahara, and to his close collaborator Kanze, who often says, "If you have in mind to preserve tradition it is not worth preserving."

But almost any artist working today in Japan is mindful of the tormenting issue of the way his work will be perceived, both in Japan and in the world at large. Some artists do battle with those in their own culture who persist in maintaining unexamined platitudes about what is Japanese in Japanese art, while others declare themselves firmly within certain Japanese traditions. The well-known Japanese sculptor Toshikatsu Endō insists that "Zen Buddhist concepts permeate Japanese culture,"[9] while the composer Takemitsu seeks always to find cognates in Western culture for the aesthetic principles of Zen. Some artists stubbornly insist that certain aesthetic responses, such as the much discussed medieval notion of *mono no aware* (variously defined as "pathos," or, as Donald Richie says, "the transience of all earthly things, a concept popularized by Buddhism and of great importance in any discussion of Japanese aesthetics"[10]) are peculiar to Japanese art and culture. Others throw their hands up in despair when that old fixation is brought up.

The fact that Westerners have accepted certain Japanese truisms, such as that the Japanese are closer to Nature than others, sometimes irritates contemporary artists, some of whom were only too glad to be represented in a traveling exhibition of Japanese art provocatively titled, "Against Nature." But others try to sustain references to nature in their work while rejecting claims to exclusivity. Teshigahara, for instance, found affinities with the Spaniard Gaudí's approach to nature and was inspired to formulate his views within his own Japanese context. Yet, he is well aware of the snares awaiting an artist who ignores the constricting effects of views that posit a uniqueness in Japanese art, or who accepts certain Western demands for Japanism—demands, paradoxically, often set up by the Japanese themselves, who are frequently most ambivalent on the subject.

Shadows, too often reminiscent of the fascist past, hover behind the arguments of Japanese uniqueness, or discussions of "Oriental" versus "Western" views of existence. Even Suzuki slips into characterizations of the "Asian" mind that defy evidence of great disparities between Indian, Chinese, and Japanese points of view. Most Japanese artists and intellectuals respond with exasperation to sweeping characterizations, and above all, Western reports on the special characteristics of Japan.

When Roland Barthes published *The Empire of Signs*, his essay on what he called Japan, but really, on Barthes' very selective emotional responses to things Japanese, even his ardent admirers in contemporary Japan were disappointed. Barthes' rhapsodic flights, sometimes bordering on the absurd, such as when he calls the hand of the Pachinko player that of an artist, could not fail to remind his Japanese readers of the bitter truth that Westerners all too often invent a *Mikado* and *Madame Butterfly* rather than have real encounters with Japanese culture. As an example of Barthes' fantasies, there is his disquisition on chopsticks:

By chopsticks, food becomes no longer a prey to which one does violence (meat, flesh, over which one does battle) but a substance harmoniously transferred; they transform the previously divided substance into bird food, and rice into a flow of milk; maternal, they tirelessly perform the gesture which creates the mouthful, leaving our alimentary manners, armed with pikes and knives, that of predation.[11]

The passage from Barthes may be compared with Isozaki's passage on chopsticks in his essay on *ma* in which he carefully locates differences between Japanese and Western conceptions of space and time:

Originally the word *hashi* referred not only to a bridge but also to an edge, chopsticks, steps, etc. The word *hashi* did not mean a specific thing but rather implied a bridging of Ma (space between two objects). An "edge" represented the limit of one world, assuming the existence of another world beyond. Anything that crossed, filled, or projected into the chasm of Ma (space between two edges) was designated *hashi*. The "edges" bridged might include, for example, the secular world and the heavenly world; the upper level and the lower level; the plate and the mouth (there is a homophone *hashi* in the Japanese language that means chopsticks, an instrument that bridges the Ma between the plate and the mouth) . . . [12]

Here what Nishida called "historic actuality" prevails, lending a believable dimension to the concept of *ma* as a specifically Japanese phenomenon.

Perplexing issues attendant on discerning specifics in Japanese culture serve often as goads to contemporary Japanese artists. They are perpetually on guard against the trite formulations of what is termed *Nihonjin-ron*, the tendency amongst ordinary Japanese to see themselves as unique. In a deliberately provocative book titled *The Myth of Japanese Uniqueness*, Peter N. Dale discusses many of the concepts the Japanese customarily attribute exclusively to themselves, among them *mono no aware*, which he says is used "to escape the analytic lenses of foreigners."[13] It is Dale's contention that many of the locutions that the Japanese regard as impossible for foreigners to comprehend were sponsored during the Meiji period for nationalistic ends. Even so brilliant an intellectual as Tanizaki slipped into the habit during the fascist years. He cites a passage from Tanizaki's *Bunshō tokuhon*:

> Our nation's language (*kokugo*) bears an unalienable relationship with our national character (*kokuminsei*), and the fact that Japanese is poor in vocabulary does not necessarily mean that our culture is inferior to that of the West or China. Rather it is proof that chatting (*oshaberi*) is not a part of our national character.[14]

The thrust of Dale's book is to demonstrate that the institutional forms of *Nihonjin-ron* reflect deliberate totalitarian strategies. He attempts to show that during the years immediately before the Second World War, the fascists coined slogans of uniqueness that, worked over in great profusion and with considerable intellectual agility, were very useful in maintaining totalitarian control. The implications in most Japanese writing are: that the Japanese are a distinctly homogenous people; that they have special sensibilities that enable them to communicate with each other on levels Westerners will never understand; and that there can be no parallels in Western countries.

Vestiges of such thinking remain quite active in contemporary Japan and are deplored by many Japanese intellectuals who lament that the self-image of the people is still fixed in these old and dangerously nationalistic myths. If one doubts Dale's observations—and they were hotly disputed—one can turn to a very different kind of book written by someone far removed from the intellectual milieu. In fact, Peregrine Hodson's verbatim account of his experience in a Japanese investment banking firm is an astonishing confirmation of Dale's argument. Hodson early in his book quotes his boss:

> We Japanese can know each other's minds. We are a homogenous society: same schools, same universities, same culture, same language, same minds. *Mondo nai*, no problem.[15]

Soon after, at an office party, a co-worker discourses on drinking:

> Biologically we are different from other people . . . We Japanese have different guts from foreigners. It has been proved

scientifically. And our center of gravity is in a different place. And our brains are different. That is why we Japanese are so close to nature.[16]

At still another party, there was a discussion of *ishin-denshin*, which one woman said was like telepathy, only different. Hodson observes:

It was one of those parties when every conversation is a *Nihonjin-ron*, why are the Japanese so Japanese? Does a person have to be Japanese to understand the Japanese? And is Japan different from the rest of the world or is the rest of the world different from Japan?[17]

Although the conversations Hodson records would not be likely, at least not in such caricatural form in the circles frequented by Teshigahara, they do reflect a current of conventional thought that is still well ensconced and that could not fail to irritate more subtle minds. In fact, in more refined terms, these attitudes turn up even in the artistic milieu, as when one of the curators of the touring exhibition "Against Nature," Shinji Kōmoto, declares that the Japanese language is not analytical and that, "When a Japanese person faces an impressive landscape he simply describes exclamatorily how impressive it is; he does not try to analyze it or to order its attributes."[18] Any writer familiar with Japanese literary history could counter with many passages disputing Kōmoto's generalization.

An artist such as Teshigahara could, and did, in his own work, interpret the past of Japanese art in wholly different terms from Kōmoto, who maintained that traditional art "was related to style as a mode of living which results in Formality."[19] Kōmoto confidently asserted that artworks for traditional Japanese artists operated as elements to create a particular space or mood, were not "personal artistic statements, and were not a method of defining meaning and ideas."[20] Teshigahara had early discovered, already when he made his first film on Hokusai, that easy generalizations such as these can hardly cover the complexities of Japanese art history—a history that includes the presence in every generation of the *itan*, the heretical figure who challenges all generalizations and strikes out on his own, making distinctive personal artistic statements. It is not difficult to understand why Teshigahara embraced so enthusiastically the paradoxes implicit in Okamoto's philosophy, wholly committed to dismantling old prejudices through the assault on what he ironically called "common sense."

If Teshigahara for the past few years has been reinventing a past, he does not pander to the *Nihonjin-ron* mentality. His is a thoughtful attempt to draw upon legitimate history not as myth but as a body of diverse facts having the power to engage the mind. His Rikyū could be any artist entangled in the toils of politics and power. In the light of the dilemmas vouchsafed by intellectuals since the Meiji era, Teshigahara and his comrades in arts had to struggle to maintain a balance. It was not easy to find equilibrium amongst such well-rehearsed contradictions. These artists, whose situation was very much like that of the early Russian avant-garde, responded by insisting on variety, on freedom to pursue multiple courses, on the right to seek grand fusions of ideas in total works of art. Just as some Russians had envisioned a plenitude of attitudes—the artist and graphic designer Iliazd, for instance, who in 1913 founded a short-lived movement called *Vsechestvo*, meaning "everythingism," that would "use and combine all the forms of art in the past"—Japanese artists responded to their culture and its conflicting demands with an aesthetic adventurism that recognized no bounds.

Teshigahara has moved about in the various arts—film, ikebana, pottery, calligraphy, opera, theater, and landscape architecture—in an indefatigable quest for the delicate thread that joins past with present, tradition with innovations. There seems to have been an instinctive quest for continuity, even within vanguard traditions. His great esteem for Okamoto led him to an intense examination of Surrealist principles, not the least of which was the Surrealist conviction that the origins of the arts, so distant in time, were pristine, more expressive, and universal. Breton had waxed ecstatic when he encountered works from preliterate cultures.

Perhaps the twentieth-century's obsession with primitive cultures was a result of its great disappointments in modern culture. Certainly the century has seen endless recapitulations of the rediscovery of the primordial. And often, the most intense inquiries into the arts of early peoples have occurred after cataclysmic public events as when the post-Hiroshima generation in Japan turned back to the Jōmon culture.

The desire to go back to beginnings when everything was new is one of the distinguishing characteristics of modern artistic culture, and

Teshigahara has followed this desire in many of his undertakings. Although by nature he recoils from the more violent aspects of the quest—he clearly prefers Noh to Butoh—he shares, even with artists of the Butoh formation, many views. For instance, the views of Ushio Amagatsu, founder of the Sankai Juku troupe, who has said of his 1982 composition, *Homage to Jōmon*, that it is far from being uniquely Japanese, and that he finds clear similarities in the Neolithic vestiges in the south of France, northern Spain, or pre-Columbian America, that send us back to communal roots, "a universal type of dialogue between man and the object":

> But the fact that one body is Asiatic while another is American or European, while it may inevitably affect the purely corporal aspect of the dance, does not exclude the fact that the same thought can inhabit dancers from different climates: diverse natures produce diverse cultures, but each, when completely integrated, ends always by sending us back to human nature and the universe . . . [21]

When Teshigahara insists that fundamental human problems never change, his position—both artistic and philosophical—is clear. He seeks imaginative means to enunciate his basic humanistic convictions in all the arts, and is what Westerners would call "a Renaissance man." His native character is optimistic, impulsive, and gregarious, and while he is capable of sustained scholarly work, as in his Gaudí film, he often prefers spontaneous and ephemeral performances.

Journalists are fond of citing his spate of interests—racing cars, boxing, high cuisine—and of noting his distinctive dress, bordering on dandyism. Fairly often, Teshigahara does wear elegant clothes designed by the imaginative designer Issey Miyake, who thinks of Teshigahara as "curiosity itself." Miyake understands Teshigahara's basic drive "to cut himself away from the tangle of rules and established styles in Japan," and says Teshigahara has achieved perfect mastery in his films above all. Another old friend, the painter Sadamasa Motonaga, characterizes Teshigahara as an adventurer with positive instincts. "Unlike so many artists in the 1950s, who felt that one step ahead and you walk straight into darkness, Hiroshi always felt that one step ahead and you walk straight into light." Motonaga, like Teshigahara, has taken to heart the fundamental Surrealist attitudes toward the natural creative endowments of all humanity, and esteems the spontaneous elements in Teshigahara's art—his play with the ephemeral, as in the bamboo environments—as his highest achievements.

Teshigahara's characteristic material sensuousness is well served by Surrealist attitudes, in which all the senses were honored in synthetic works. Throughout his career Teshigahara has worked with startling material juxtapositions and has characterized in his art the essential nature of each material: sand, its color and light, its granular character, its constant metamorphosis, its insistence on slipping out of form; bamboo, its spectacular growth, its pliable erectness, its supple jointed structure, its sounds in the wind, from sighing to clacking, and above all, its toughness, already celebrated in the ninth century by a poet who spoke of "the tough bamboo weed."[22]

Like all Surrealists, Teshigahara relishes the fortuitous encounter. Some of his works have been responses to requests from others or accidental meetings with inspiring strangers (who rapidly become friends), while others may be seen as responses to specific historical circumstances. Over the years, Teshigahara has won the kind of freedom advocated by the mentors of his youth—a freedom from the shibboleths of custom, local demands, and even from the clichés of vanguardism.

NOTES

1   Hiroaki Saitō, "Conversation with Ōoka," *Mainichi Daily News*.

2   Fujiwara Seika, *Sources of Japanese Tradition*, p. 338.

3   Daisetz Suzuki, *Zen and Japanese Culture*, p. 220.

4   Kitarō Nishida, "The Problem of Japanese Culture," in *Sources of Japanese Tradition*, p. 353.

5   Ibid., p. 353.

6   Hide Ishiguro, "La Philosophie: Eurocentrisme et exotisme des ïdées" in vol. 2, *Mots et Choses* pp. 173–197, cf. *L'Esprit de l'Europe* in 3 vols., edit. Antoine Compugnon & Jacques Seebacher, Flammarion, Paris, 1993, p. 182.

7   Ibid., p. 13.

8   Ibid., p. 14.

9 Toshikatsu Endō, statement in catalogue for the exhibition, "The Primal Spirit," 1990.

10 Donald Richie, *A Lateral View*, p. 170.

11 Roland Barthes, *Empire of Signs*, trans. Richard Howard, New York, 1982, p. 18.

12 Arata Isozaki, *Ma, Space-Time in Japan*, New York, n.d.

13 Peter N. Dale, *The Myth of Japanese Uniqueness*, p. 65.

14 Ibid., p. 79.

15 Peregrine Hodson, *A Circle Round the Sun: A Foreigner in Japan, Inc.*, New York, 1993, pp. 19–20.

16 Ibid., pp. 39–40.

17 Ibid., p. 134.

18 Shinji Kōmoto, essay in catalogue, *Against Nature*, 1989.

19 Ibid.

20 Ibid.

21 Interview with Daniel DeBruyker in *Alternatives Théâtrales*, Nos. 22–23, April–May, 1985, p. 89.

22 Minamoto no Hitoshi (880–951), in *The Little Treasury of One Hundred People, One Poem Each*, compiled by Fujiwara no Sadaie (1162–1241), trans. Tom Galt, Princeton, 1982.

INDEX

PHOTO CREDITS

Color

Page 17, photography by Nabe Studio, Inc., provided by Sogetsu Shuppan Inc.; pages 18, 19, provided by Sogetsu-kai Foundation; page 20, photography by Chūkyō Ozawa, provided by Sogetsu Shuppan Inc.; pages 22, 23, photography by Hiromi Tsuchida, provided by Sogetsu-kai Foundation; pages 24, 25, photography by Shigeo Anzai, provided by Sogetsu Shuppan Inc.; page 26, photography by Sanmu Sato, provided by Sogetsu Shuppan Inc.; page 27, photography by G.T.G., provided by Sogetsu Shuppan Inc.; page 28, photography by Takeshi Fujimori, provided by Sogetsu-kai Foundation; page 30, photography by Chūkyō Ozawa, provided by Sogetsu Shuppan Inc.; page 32, photography by Nabe Studio Inc., provided by Sogetsu Shuppan Inc.

Black and White

Pages 13, 14, provided by Teshigahara Productions Inc.; page 36, provided by Sogetsu-kai Foundation; page 45, photography by Hiroshi Teshigahara, provided by Sogetsu-kai Foundation; page 48, provided by Sogetsu Shuppan Inc.; page 51, photography by Seiji Ōtsuji, provided by Kuniharu Akiyama; page 69, provided by Teshigahara Productions, Inc.; page 71, photography by Hiroshi Teshigahara, provided by Sogetsu-kai Foundation; page 72, photography by Hiroshi Teshigahara, provided by Sogetsu-kai Foundation; page 80 (top), photography by Yasuhiro Yoshioka, provided by Sogetsu-kai Foundation; page 80 (bottom), photography by Masaaki Sekitani, provided by Sogetsu-kai Foundation; page 84, provided by Sogetsu Shuppan Inc.; pages 89, 90, 97, 99, 100, provided by Teshigahara Productions, Inc.; page 103, photography by Shōzō Kitadai, provided by Kuniharu Akiyama; page 105, photography by Kuniharu Akiyama; page 115, photography by Hiroshi Teshigahara, provided by Sogetsu-kai Foundation; page 121, provided by Teshigahara Productions, Inc.; page 126, provided by Sogetsu Shuppan Inc.; page 128, provided by Sogetsu-kai Foundation; page 132, photography by Hiromi Tsuchida, provided by Sogetsu-kai Foundation; pages 133, 134, provided by Sogetsu-kai Foundation; page 136, provided by Tokyo National Museum; pages 137, 138, provided by Sogetsu-kai Foundation; page 140, provided by Shinjuan, Daitokuji; page 146, photography by Masaaki Sekitani, provided by Sogetsu Shuppan Inc.; page 154, provided by Sen Sōsa Collection; page 154 (bottom left), provided by Tokyo National Museum; page 154, provided by The Tokugawa Art Museum; page 155, provided by Tokyo National Museum; pages 157, 160–61, provided by Teshigahara Productions, Inc.; page 169, photography by Kōzō Sekiya, provided by Sogetsu Shuppan Inc.; page 173, photography by Shigeo Anzai, provided by Sogetsu Shuppan Inc.; page 178, photography by Sogetsu Shuppan Inc., provided by Sogetsu Shuppan Inc.; pages 180, 182 (top), photography by Shigeo Anzai, provided by Sogetsu Shuppan Inc.; page 182 (bottom), photography by Ikuo Yamashita, provided by Sogetsu-kai Foundation; page 184, photography by Shigeo Anzai, provided by Sogetsu Shuppan Inc.